The SHAKESPEARE MYTH

Will Shaksper (later called Shakespeare) was born in the rural English town of Stratford-upon-Avon, in 1564. His father, John (glover, butcher, town official) and mother, Mary (a farmer's daughter) were uneducated and illiterate. Will learned to read and write, attended Stratford Grammar (grade) School, saw a few plays performed by traveling companies, then became an apprentice butcher to his father.

At eighteen, Will married twenty-six year old Anne Hathaway. Six months later their daughter, Susanna was born and two years later their twins, Judith and Hamnet were born. Sometime after his twentieth birthday Will Shaksper, running from a deer poaching incident, left his family to make his way to London.

The Mystery Years – In his twenties, Shaksper spent five to seven years in London (sans family), insinuated himself as an actor into an acting company (despite his provincial dialect and lack of experience), became a part-time play reviser / playwright (which was even lower paid and more despised than minimum wage acting / vagabonding) and acquired the professional skills (stagecraft, command of the London dialect, an extraordinary 30,000 word vocabulary, access to Court, travel, life experience, wide book-learning and the research tool of an extensive library) which enabled him to write the early 'Shakespeare' plays.

In 1593, Shaksper printed his first poem, *Venus and Adonis* (a polished effort of approximately 1,200 lines), in order to convince the younger Earl of Southampton to become his patron. Young Southampton became Shaksper's patron to the tune of £1,000 (a $250,000 plus gift today).

The following year, Shaksper became an actor-sharer (part owner) of the newly formed Chamberlain's Men (the future premier London acting company. Then came the 'golden years' (1594-1603) when the bulk of the 'Shakespeare' plays were completed. The provincial ugly duckling of Stratford became the sweet *Swan-of-Avon*.

After 1604, Will's acting slowed down / stopped, play-writing diminished and Shaksper retired to Stratford-upon-Avon. Will died in 1616, was buried under a hastily engraved stone and was left unheralded until the 1620s. A monument was then placed in Trinity Church, Stratford and the *First Folio* (of 1623) printed. The *First Folio* included thirty-eight of thirty-nine plays attributed to 'Shakespeare' (seventeen of them printed for the first time).

All of the preceding has been explained as a product of intuitive genius. The 'Shakespeare' plays, a virtual 'Encyclopedia Elizabetheana,' are said to be the result of intuition (that is intuitive genius), rather than education, life experience and access to the best minds and hearts of the age!

Myth making has been encouraged by the paucity of original documents. There are no play manuscripts, poetry manuscripts, letters by Shaksper, literary letters to Shaksper, or contemporary literary anecdotes about Shaksper. All that exist are six varying Shaksper signatures from three legal documents.

Such is the duckling to swan, poor boy to national treasure myth. Believe it if you will. If not, read on.

WHO WERE

SHAKE-SPEARE?

the ultimate who-dun-it!

Ron Allen

Silverado
San Diego, California

SILVERADO
3841 Fourth Ave., Suite 300
San Diego, CA 92103

First Edition

Printed in the United States of America on acid-free paper.

Library of Congress Cataloging-in-Publication
Allen, Ron, 1938-
        Who was Shake-speare? : the ultimate who-dun-it! /
by Ron Allen. – 1st ed.
                p.   cm.
        Includes bibliographical references and index.
ISBN 1- 891083-00-7 (pbk.)
        1. Shakespeare, William, 1565-1616—Authorship.   I. Title.
        2. Oxford, Edward De Vere, Earl of, 1550-1604—Authorship.
        3. Shakespeare, William, 1565-1616—Study and teaching.
        4. Theater—England—History—16th century.
        5. Dramatists, English—Early modern, 1500-1700—Biography.
PR2939.M36   1998
822.33   97-069058
                                                        CIP

CONTENTS

FIGURES AND ILLUSTRATIONS

ACKNOWLEDGEMENTS

With many thanks . . .

To all the people who have provided encouragement, feedback, and constant support – Dr. David Luisi, Robert Harner, Dr. Robert Bacalski, Roberta Baron, Dr. Marvin Salzberg, Ellen Salzberg, Dr. Z. Micah Kaplan, Tony Harvell, Dr. Sheldon Rashba, Denis Jana, Dr. Mel Freilicher and Marcy Meyer.

To James Berry and Pricilla Anchondo for their careful reading, editing and constructive comments.

To the knowledgeable staff at the San Diego Public Library, UCSD Library, USD Library, and the use of their facilities and materials including on-line access to major world institutions.

To The Scripteasers organization and members whose interest in theater and Shake-speare have been an impetus for the research on this project.

To my wife Sybil, daughter Laura and son Philip for their constantly affectionate spirit.

x

PREFACE

One hundred plus candidates (over centuries) have been proposed as the mythic William Shakepeare's ghost-writer. People of substance and discernment, not crazies, have grappled with the thorny question, "Who really wrote the plays and poems of Shake-speare?" A list of some who have doubted the mythic Shake-speare follows:

```
A LIST OF QUESTIONERS

Mark Twain
Sigmund Freud
Justice Harry A. Blackmun
Charlie Chaplin
Ralph Waldo Emerson
Orson Welles
Walt Whitman
Malcolm X
Otto von Bismarck
Benjamin Disraeli
Daphne DuMaurier
John Galsworthy
Senator Paul Douglas
Clifton Fadiman
Charles DeGaulle
James Joyce
Helen Keller
John Greenleaf Whittier
Samuel Taylor Coleridge
Thomas Hardy
Oliver Wendell Holmes
James Russell Lowell
```

1. A List of Questioners.

Who Were Shake-speare? unmasks the two collaborators who shared the pen name William Shake-
speare, how and why this came about, and explores
the sometime involvement of their creative cronies.
'Who Were' also re-evaluates the role of Will
Shaksper of Stratford-upon-Avon. Yes, Shaksper
was there! Yes, he did actively participate!

2. Hamlet by William Shake-speare (1603).

To accomplish the preceding requires sweeping away centuries of scholarly and popular myth-making, eliminating repeatedly reprinted half-truths, and discarding unsupported assumptions / erroneous speculations about Shake-speare. What emerges is a radiant picture of collaborative genius in the remarkable Elizabethan era.

SHAKSPER * SHAKE-SPEARE * SHAKESPEARE

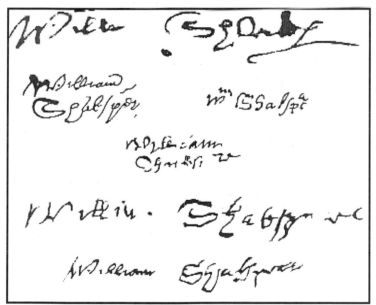

3. The six Shaksper signatures (with the surname spelled as follows – *Shackper, Shakspear, Shakspea., Shackspere* and *Shakspeare* – but no Shak̲espeare).

Three of the above signatures are from Shaksper's '*Will*' (1616), two are from the deed / indenture to the purchased house in Blackfriar's (1613), and one is from the deposition in the Belott-Mountjoy case (1612). This is all we have of Shaksper's handwriting, unless he personally drafted his own *Last Will and Testament*.

For clarity, the family name **Shaksper** is used to refer to William Shaksper of Stratford-upon-Avon; while the hyphenated name **Shake-speare** is used when referring to the works, pen name or literary aspects of the author(s') life.

The family name of William Shaksper of Stratford-upon-Avon was spelled in various ways, but the first syllable was pronounced in the sixteenth century as 'Shacks' or 'Shax,' as it was sometimes spelled, followed by 'per' (pair). The second syllable was sometimes written as 'bere.' Could Shagsbere have been pronounced shag-sbere? No. The Shaksper signatures reflect how the Stratford man used and pronounced his name during his life.

The hyphenated name Shake-speare (a compound of two words) appeared regularly in approximately half of the early editions of the *Bard's* plays and poems as well as in early anecdotes and references. Early editions of works (whether hyphenated or not) did not drop the 'e' in the first syllable(s) of Shake-speare, as did almost anything pertaining to Shaksper-of-Stratford's private life.

Why the hyphen in Shake-speare? Reasons that come to mind are:

1. In the sixteenth century, the name Shake-speare might have been pronounced (without hyphen) as Shak-es-pair or Shakes-pair. Adding the hyphen precluded this pronunciation.

2. The hyphenated name accentuated allusions to spears and shaking. This would have appealed to literary minds and hinted at a pen name.

Until 1598, all Shake-speare works were published anonymously. *Venus and Adonis* (1593) and *Lucrece* (1594) had 'William Shakespeare' dedications, but no author on the title page.

Elizabethan spelling was variable, but names were not hyphenated unless they were:

1. Place names such as White-friar's.

2. It was the author's (person's) idiosyncrasy to hyphenate his/her name, as did writer Charles Fitz-Geffrey and publisher Edward All-de.

3. The hyphenated name came down from earlier times when surnames were introduced. An example is the name Old-castle.

4. The name was invented, or was a fictional name which played on words. The play name and character, *Sir John Old-castle* qualify this way.

The very first reference to the name Shake-speare appeared in the commentary verse to *Willobie his Advisa* (Anonymous, 1594). The lines follow:

> "Yet Tarquyne plucks his glistening grape,
> And **Shake-speare**, paints poor Lucrece rape."

In the sixteenth century, 'shake' and 'shak' (shack) were spoken differently. Each word differed as well in meaning. Per Helge Kokeritz in *Shake-speare's Pronunciation*, the word 'shack' would have our current pronunciation, while the 'a' in 'Shake' would sound like the 'ie' in lie. Elizabethans pronounced Shake-speare as 'Shiek-spair.'

The Oxford English Dictionary defines 'shack' as, "Grain fallen from the ear and available for the feeding of pigs, poultry, etc., after the harvest..." This definition is followed by samples of usage in 1536 and 1563. We have glimpsed at the signatures of a man who signed and pronounced his name **Shaksper** (Shaxpair), and printed works bearing the name **Shake-speare** (Shiek-spair). This discrepancy is no accident. It is one loose thread that when further pulled, will help unravel the authorship mystery.

On to *Who Were Shake-speare?* So dear reader, sit back, peruse and enjoy. May you find as much delight in the revelations about *'Who Were'* as I did in probing these murky secrets of a past age.

Ron Allen

Point to ponder:

1. Many reputable thinkers have doubted the standard myth; that Will Shaksper, poor boy from the provinces (with modest education and much elbow grease to earn his keep), became sole-moneyed-creator of the world's greatest dramatic works and the finest examples of English language poetry – a veritable 'Encyclopedia Elizabetheana' – all through intuitive genius.

INTRODUCTION

Shake-speare, you devil! You've led scholars and fans on a merry madcap romp for over 400 years. The famous, the serious, the learned and even the kooks argue about who wrote your plays and poetry; what you said, what you meant; what people have said about you; who you plagiarized from, who plagiarized you; etc. It goes on *ad nauseum*.

Who Were Shake-speare? exposes the dynamic duo who co-wrote the plays, their sometime creative cronies, and provides background on how it all came about.

There is no record or copy of the earliest Shake-speare work(s). They were written and performed sometime in the 1580s, or earlier. There are no handwritten autographs of any Shake-speare plays or poems; not a one. There are no letters Shake-speare wrote to anyone (literary or otherwise). There is not one scrap of literary correspondence to Shake-speare from friends and admirers. No one dedicated a work to Shake-speare while the author(s) lived. At Shake-speare's death(s) no eulogies to 'W. S.' were penned.

Why have those who knew you, shared your thoughts, friendship and intimacy kept so silent; silent about you, Shake-speare? Those who knew you left not one contemporary anecdote, not a shred of light to illumine the corporeal William Shake-speare.

Very mysterious. Very shadowy. Very suspicious. Very unlike other 16th century authors, even minor ones.

Yes! Signatures, letters, autographs, friendly and unfriendly anecdotes and educational information exist on most of the well known poets, translators, playwrights and writers of Shake-speare's time. Check out your local library for *British Authors Before 1800* by Kunitz and Haycraft. Biographies, schooling and anecdotes on Shake-speare's contemporaries such as the following are included:

```
                ELIZABETHAN WRITERS
    Beaumont, Francis (1584-1616) ❖+
    Chapman, George (1559-1634) (❖?)
    Chettle, Henry (1560- 1607) ?
    Dekker, Thomas (1572?-1632) ?
    Donne, John (1573?-1631) ❖+
    Drayton, Michael (1563-1631) ?
    Fletcher, John (1579-1625) ❖
    Greene, Robert (1558-1592) ◎
    Heywood, Thomas (1574-1641) ❖
    Jonson, Ben (1572-1637) *(♦honorary degrees)
    Kyd, Thomas (1558-1594) *
    Lodge, Thomas (1558?-1625) ◎+
    Lyly, John (1554-1606) ◎
    Marlowe, Christopher (1564-1593) ◎
    Marston, John (1574-1634) ◎+
    Munday, Anthony (1553-1633) *
    Nashe, Thomas (1567-1601) ◎
    Oxford, Edward, Lord (1550-1604) ◎(+?)
    Peele, George (1558?-1597?) ◎
    Raleigh, Sir Walter (1582?-1618) ❖+
    Sidney, Sir Philip (1554-1586) ❖
    Spencer, Edmund (-1599) ◎
```

4.   Elizabethan Writers (*=grammar school, ❖=college, ♦=degree, ◎=post- grad, +=law inn, ?=unclear, __='University Wits' — (1580s playwrights).

With very little effort, I was able to find and photocopy handwriting facsimiles of these authors. This included signatures of fifteen, and the letters or autographs of fourteen. More are undoubtedly available.

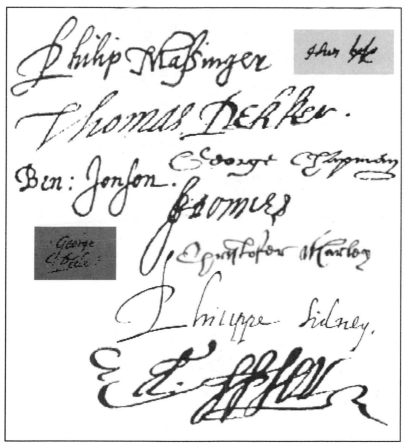

5. Signature Samples — Writers.

Shake-speare, though a most prominent author of his age, mysteriously lacks any contemporary Elizabethan biography or documents relating to his literary life. Was Shake-speare a nobody; an unknown author in

Elizabethan times? Hardly! Shake-speare's work was famous during the authors' time. The plays were the toast of London. They were often presented by provincial and touring London acting companies. Shake-speare experienced firsthand the numerous reprintings of *Venus and Adonis* (ten editions) and *The Rape of Lucrece* (three editions). W.S.'s work was well known and admired. Many 16th century authors borrowed, quoted, mimicked and imitated the *Bard's* poetry and plays.

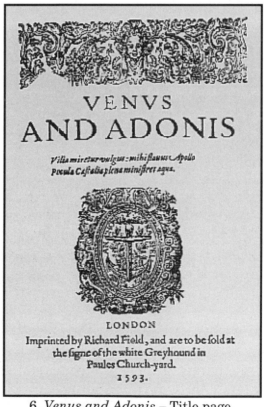

6. *Venus and Adonis* – Title page.

John Q. Adams, Folger Shakespeare Library Director wrote, "When the poem *(Venus and Adonis)* was still all the rage, there was entered in the Stationers' Register, on May 17, 1594, a close imitation by one 'T.H.', with the same theme of unrequited love, approximately the same plot, the same setting, the same richly ornate style, and with the title *Oenone and Paris,* parallel to the title *Venus and Adonis...* Throughout the text, verbal plagiarism of Shakespeare's poem is everywhere conspicuous."

Yes, *Oenone and Paris* poked fun at the Shake-speare *Venus and Adonis* dedication, and describes imitating the Greek painter Apelles' method of concealing authorship. Most of the amusing dedication follows:

> Curteous Readers... Here you have the first fruits of my endeavors and maidenhead of my pen; which, how rude and unpolished it may seem in your eagle-sighted eyes, I can not conceive, and therefore, fearing the worst, I have sought in some sort to prevent it. Apelles having framed any work of worth, would set it openly to the view of all, hiding himself closely in a corner of the workhouse... In the publishing of this little poem, I have imitated the painter, giving you this poor pamphlet to peruse, lurking in the meanwhile obscurely till that, hearing how you please to censure of my simple work, I may in some other *Opere magis elaborato* apply my vein to your humours...

Some viewed Shake-speare's name for the first time in the dedication of *Venus and Adonis* (1593), to Henry, Earl of Southampton. Like the Greek painter Apelles in the humorous *Oenone,* Shake-speare describes his concealed authorship in his dedication which reads in part:

> "... But if the first **heir** of my **invention** prove deformed, I shall be sorie it had so noble a god-father."

Before discussing these critical lines, let's look at the *Oxford English Dictionary* (OED) definitions of 'heir' and 'invention.'

> HEIR... 3. *fig.* That which is begotten; offspring ; product. *Obs.* ... **1593** SHAKS. Ven. & Ad. Ded., Dedicating my unpolished lines to your Lordship. . But if the first heire of my inuention proue deformed, I shall be sorry it had so noble a God-Father.

> INVENTION...I. The action, faculty, or manner of inventing... II. The thing invented. 6. Something devised... **1593** SHAKS. 3 *Henry VI*, iv. I. 35 What if both Lewis and Warwick be appeas'd, By such inuention as I can devise?... 8. A fictitious statement or story; a fabrication, fiction, figment... **1601** SHAKS. *All's Well* III. vi. 105 None in the world, but returne with inuention, and clap vpon you two or three probable lies...

Shake-speare, in the plays and poems, uses the word 'invention' thirty-two times, and the word 'heir' one hundred fifty-two times. Using a Shake-speare search engine on the Internet, one can peruse how the *Bard* used these two words. All of Shake-speare's uses of the words 'heir' and 'invention' fit within the dictionary definitions of these words. That being the case, we should be able to substitute equivalent words in the quotation without altering meaning.

The dictionary alternatives able to be substituted for 'my invention' are 'my inventive faculty,' 'my imagination' or 'my invented device' (pen name). A poem <u>cannot</u> <u>inherit</u> an inventive faculty or imagination. A poem is the product, not the heir of imagination or invention. 'My invented device' (pen name) is the only correct use of 'invention' in the phrase under discussion.

Charlton Ogburn, in *The Mysterious William Shakespeare*, states the following:

> On the other hand, if "my invention" is an invented name, the poem that appears under it can very well be said to have inherited it. A name above all is what an offspring does inherit. "William Shakespeare" was evidently recognized at once as a pseudonym.

The word 'first' is also used in the phrase "first heir of my invention." In this dedication, for the first time in print, we see the name 'William Shakespeare.' This is possibly the first use of the name in this format. **The author** (pen name) **is not printed on the title page.**

To paraphrase the line under discussion, 'The first heir' (poem which is first product) 'of my invention' (my invented name), or, **if this poem which is the first product of my pen name (Shake-speare), is deformed, I apologize, Southampton.**

We don't know when Shake-speare's first poetry was written. Documentation of Shake-speare's literary

legacy began in **1593**, with the printing of the poem
Venus and Adonis. This polished effort of approximately 1,200 lines was hardly a first attempt. What
preceded *'Venus?'* We don't know what play(s) of
Shake-speare were produced before *Titus Andronicus*
and *Henry IV, pt. 2* (both printed in **1594**). When was
'Titus' written? Perhaps in the late 1580's, or perhaps
earlier? The play was performed by several acting
companies over the years before ever being printed.

After **1594**, in spurts through **1622**, seventeen more
plays and three works containing 'W. S.' poetry and
sonnets were printed. The posthumous *First Folio* of
1623 included seventeen plays, printed for the first
time, plus an additional eighteen plays which were
previously printed. *Pericles* (printed in 1609) did not
appear in the *First Folio* (for copyright problems?).

Shake-speare wrote and collaborated on additional
plays; some of which are unknown / lost, such as *Love's
Labour's Won*, and some which are disputed, such as
Sir Thomas More. Over the millenia, scholars have
speculated that Shake-peare wrote and/or co-wrote the
plays: *The Famous Victories of Henry V, The Two
Noble Kinsmen, Edward III, Edmund Ironsides,
Thomas of Woodstock* and the lost (though possibly, re-
cently rediscovered) play, *Cardenio. Duke Humphrey,
Iphis and Ianth,* and *King Stephen* (lost plays) were
entered in the *Stationers' Register* as Shake-speare's
work. Scholars have also speculated on the *Bard's*
authorship of additional poetic works ranging from the
'Phaeton' sonnet to *The Funeral Elegy* (1612).

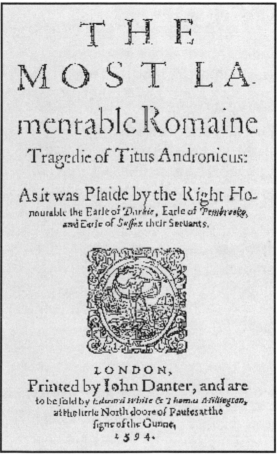

THE
MOST LA-
mentable Romaine
Tragedie of Titus Andronicus:

As it was Plaide by the Right Ho-
nourable the Earle of *Darbie*, Earle of *Pembrooke*,
and Earle of *Suffex* their Seruants.

LONDON,
Printed by Iohn Danter, and are
to be fold by *Edward White* & *Thomas Millington,*
at the litrle North doore of Paules at the
figne of the Gunne,
1 5 9 4.

7. *Titus Andronicus* (1594 – sans author).

Shake-speare, you are such a cornucopia! You are a
cornucopia of abundance, variety and diverse plays (in
diverse styles) with characters that encompass all of
humanity (comedies, tragedies, English histories,
Roman settings, Greek settings, current English settings, contemporary Italian settings, scenes in French,
and glimpses of the Elizabethan Court).

This cornucopia also includes epic and erotic poetry of hefty length, illuminating sonnets and possibly a funeral elegy.

The detail included in the works is fascinating, whether writing on law, politics, art, mythical animals, flowers, music performance, song lyrics, falconry, sports, bawdy humor, fat jokes, circa 1600 in-jokes, Bible quotations, descriptions of Italy / Europe, mythology, medicine, science, the ancient classics, the sea, military science, woodcraft, etc.

Who Were Shake-speare? reveals the collaborative hands that made the above possible. The talent-rich, genius-inspired writings are collectively attributed to William Shake-speare, revered as the world's greatest dramatist and celebrated as our finest English language poet.

Points to ponder:

1. More is known (documentable) about most Elizabethan writers' artistic lives / education than is known about such matters regarding Shake-speare.

2. Shake-speare's works were well known in Elizabethan times. They were quoted, mimicked and plagiarized freely. For example, Thomas Heywood borrowed liberally from Shake-speare in many of his plays.

3. Shake-speare dedicates the poem *Venus and Adonis* (1593) as 'William Shakespeare' yet leaves the title page sans author. This is the first time the *nom de plume* (variant from Shaksper) appears in print.

1. COLLABORATORS AHOY

Was the subtly altered name 'Shake-speare' an accomodation address (appellation) for collaboration? Was William Shake-speare a pen name for a dynamic writing team, consisting of William Shaksper (1564-1616) of Stratford-upon-Avon and Edward de Vere (1550-1604), 17th Earl of Oxford; plus less regularly participating artistic cronies? Fantastic? Maybe not.

A little background before exposing 'Who Were?'...

Today we idolize the sole creative genius in the arts. We prize artists / authors Picasso, Chekhov, Steinbeck, Yo-yo Ma, Nureyev, etc. Yet, ironically, possibly the greatest art form evolving out of the twentienth century, the motion picture, is a collaborative medium. As one looks back toward the Renaissance, joint efforts in the arts increase. For example, many of the painter, Rubens' works were done by his apprentices (with master touches).

The Elizabethan theater of London in the late 1500s and early 1600s was a den of collaboration.

Think of Francis Beaumont and John Fletcher, credited with fifty-two plays; although it's hard to determine which plays were co-written together, written alone by one or the other, or were co-written with others such as Philip Massinger. Fletcher's collaborative hand is proposed in Shake-speare's play, *Henry VIII. Eastward Ho* by George Chapman, Ben Jonson and John Marston was suppressed for offending (slurs on Scots) James I. *Eastward Ho* landed Chapman in a Tower of London prison cell. The Crown censors were a pretty tough lot!

All but twelve of Henry Chettle's fifty plus plays were collaborations with writers such as Ben Jonson, Anthony Munday and Michael Drayton. While Chettle received the going rate for writing a play (a modest 4 to 7 pounds) from theatrical manager Philip Henslowe, he revised one Munday play for 10 shillings. Nathaniel Rowley, John Day, Thomas Middleton, John Ford, Thomas Heywood and Thomas Dekker, in various combinations, co-authored plays. Collaborative works were produced by such teams as Robert Greene / Thomas Lodge, Thomas Middleton / Ben Jonson and Christopher Marlowe / Thomas Nashe.

The play *Sir Thomas More* (1590?) provides a unique picture of co-authorship, since much of the original handwritten manuscript exists. Scholars have argued that Shake-speare was (were?) a collaborator on this work. With laborious effort, the handwritings of six people have been found in the manuscript of *Sir Thomas More,* as follows:

Anthony Munday (original hand), Henry Chettle, Thomas Heywood, Thomas Dekker, a professional scribe (hand observed in plot of *The Seven Deadly Sins*) and an unknown hand some conjecture as Shake-speare. A committee project?

Elizabethan theatrical companies generally bought, owned and zealously guarded their plays.

8. *The Spanish Tragedy* – Title Page.

These plays were often updated to reflect the acting company cast / capabilities, current style and popular taste. The author usually had no say in how the play was altered. Only about ten percent of plays performed were published. The very popular play, *The Spanish Tragedy* (later credited to Thomas Kyd) went through nine anonymous printed editions from 1592 to 1633.

Sixteenth century society considered writing for the stage a low craft. The use of initials and pseudonyms to disguise authorship of plays, poetry and fictional works (except classical translations) was commonplace in Elizabethan times. Nobles and gentry used this stratagem to avoid the stigma of an association with the distasteful activities of theater, acting and non-classical writing.

'G. P.' for George Peele appeared on the title pages of such plays as *The Arraignment of Paris* (1584). Thomas Nashe used the pen name Cuthbert Curry-knave. An anonymous pamphleteer(s) used Martin Marprelate. Subtly changing Shaksper to Shake-speare (in print) separated the man from the work (creating a pen name).

Shake-speare was never a compound name for the 'Shake' and 'Speare' families. The scholar, E. K. Chambers researched and reported on eighty-three versions of the English family name Shaksper / Shakespeare. None were hyphenated.

In the famous, posthumous *First Folio* of 1623, we find 'Shakespeare' and 'Shake-speare.' Both appear in the dedicatory verses. The verse by 'I. M.' below offers Shake-speare. Mr. 'I. M.,' according to scholars (since Elizabethan printers used the capital letter 'I' for both 'I' and 'J'), was either John Marston, Jasper Mayne, or James Mabbe. Ma'bbe not. Perhaps I. M. was simply saying 'I. M. (I am) unknown.'

To the memorie of M. *W.Shake-speare.*

VVEE *wondred* (Shake-fpeare) *that thou went'ft fo foone
From the Worlds-Stage, to the Graues-Tyring-roome.
Wee thought thee dead, but this thy printed worth,
Tels thy Spectators, that thou went'ft but forth
To enter with applaufe. An Actors Art,
Can dye, and liue, to acte a fecond part.
That's but an* Exit *of Mortalitie;
This, a* Re-entrance *to a* Plaudite.

I. M.

9. I.M.'s *First Folio* Sonnet (1623).

One strong indication of collaboration in Shakespeare's work is **style variation within single plays**.

Writers often adopt or ape different styles during their lifetime. Masters manage to stay within one style / creative concept within a single work (even when revising or rewriting). That's why we speak of Picasso's 'blue period,' etc.

Not so for the Shake-speare plays! Shake-speare's stylistic variation (within single works) displays the multiple pens (and multiple visions) of co-authorship in writing, and in later updating / freshening the works.

In addition to style, quality varies within many Shake-speare works. A case in point is the *Sonnets*. Of the 154 sonnets, many are considered masterpieces, some fairly good, and some rather pedestrian (unworthy). The difference in quality / style of individual sonnets and the number repeating a single subject (17 urging a young man to procreate, etc.), has led some scholars to believe all the sonnets are not by the same hand. Collaborators?

So! Who were they? Patience! A bit more background.

Points to ponder:

1.   Elizabethan plays were often collaborative efforts.

2.   Stylistic diversity within a single work of acknowledged great artists is a co-authorship indicator. Some may be the product of revisions but some are the product of initial co-authorship.

3.   Quality variances within a single work (of acknowledged great artists) can be a co-authorship indicator. Such variance can easily be seen in Rubens' works. The yards of Rubens' Royal 'commissions' in the *Louvre* do not have the unity or impact of his portrait of his wife and child (in the same museum).

2. ELIZABETH ENTERTAINS

Elizabethan theater was the darling of the Queen, Court and aristocracy. Theater existed at the whim and pleasure of the royals. A London (public) theater company needed a license from the Queen, a noble licensee (patron) and an approved theater in which to perform. Only a handful of such theater companies were allowed to function at any one time.

10. An Elizabethan Playhouse.

In 1574, Leicester's Men received the initial patent which legitimized public theater companies. By 1587, the Crown assumed complete control of all London area acting companies via the Privy Council, Lord Chamberlain and Revels Office. An actor had strong incentive to seek company membership. Unaffiliated actors would be considered rogues or vagabonds ('masterless' without trade) and subject to arrest or worse (under the Statute enacted in 1572).

Of the few theater companies allowed, each vied to appear before the Queen and Court, and at other times toured the provinces (especially during closures due to plague or Crown restriction).

The Queen, through her Revel's Office (headed by a Master of the Revels), maintained her own companies of musicians, actors, costumes, scenery, etc., for on-going entertainment.

London drama performance dates back to the late 1300s, when boys' chapel actors performed religious plays. Then, as in Elizabethan times, all roles (male and female) were played by boys and men. In the 1580s, Royal Chapel children, The Children of Paul's, and Oxford's Boys (Edward de Vere's company) played together, showcasing John Lyly and other writers. These companies provided a training ground for acting and stagecraft.

Acting companies also 'amalgamated' for periods of time; that is, performed together jointly.

Enterprising theatrical managers began building public theaters to present plays, prize-fighting, bull-baiting, bear-baiting, cock fighting, etc. Some theaters such as The Swan, The Hope, The Bull Inn and The Phoenix (The Cockpit), would present a play one day and sport the next. A chronological listing of representative London area Elizabethan theater companies follows:

ELIZABETHAN THEATER COMPANIES

COMPANY	PATRON	DATES
Children of Paul's *-	St. Paul's Cathedral	1378-1606?
Children of the Chapel *-	Crown	1501-1616
Warwick's Men *+	Ambrose Dudley	1528-1580
(joined Oxford's Men in 1580)		
Strange's Men *+	Lords Derby	1550s-1594
(Derby's Men)		
Worcester's Men *+	Earls of Worcester	1555-1602
(joined Oxford's Men)		1602-1603
Leicester's Men *+	Robert Dudley	1560?-1588
Sussex's Men *+	Earls of Sussex	1569-1594
Oxford's Boys *-	Edward de Vere	1582-1591
(amalgamated with Children of Paul's, etc.)		
Oxford's Men *+	Edward de Vere	1580?-1603
Queen's Men *+	Queen Elizabeth	1583-1603
Admiral's Men *+	Charles Howard	1585-1603
Pembroke's Men -+	Henry Herbert	1592?-1597?
King's Men *-	King James	1603-1642
Queen Anne's Men *-	Queen Anne	1603-1619
Lady Elizabeth's Men	Elizabeth Stuart	1611-1615

11. Elizabethan Theater Companies - Chronologically (*=Court performances, +=provincial performances).

Actors and writers (unless they had private means) were a poor, badly thought of, exploited lot. The exceptions were the few canny manager directors like Philip Henslowe, his son-in-law Edward Alleyn (actor-cum-manager) and to a lesser extent the Burbages (theatre owners).

With all this rollicking good fun (theater, sports, etc.), it must be emphasized that Elizabethan society was decidedly authoritarian and feudal in outlook. The Queen and royals ruled the country with an iron hand under authority from God. All were subject to submit to the imperial 'We.' Theater performance days and times were regulated by the Crown, as well as holiday performance schedules. Major London Elizabethan theaters, in chronological order, included:

LONDON AREA THEATERS

Boar's Head Inn - (1557-1603)
Bull Inn - (1570's?-1596?)
The Theatre - (1576-1589)
Curtain - (1577-1660?)
Blackfriar's Theatre - (1576-1642)
Newington Butts Theater - (1579?-1596?)
Cross Keys Inn - (1579-1596?)
Bel Savage Inn - (1580's-1596?)
Rose - (1587-1622?)
Swan Theatre - (1595?-1621?)
Globe Theatre (first) - (1599-1613)
          (second) - (1614-1644)
Fortune - (1600-1621)
Red Bull - (1606-1633?)

---

12.   London Area Theaters — Chronologically.

The theater and printed works were considered important propaganda tools. A seditious play was deemed capable of causing dissention, leading to potential toppling of the monarchy.

Strict censorship was the rule. The chief censor was Thomas Whitgift (Archbishop of Canterbury from 1583-1604). Whitgift was a close friend and confidant of Queen Elizabeth. Under edict (1586), all books required approval (license) by the Archbishop of Canterbury or his deputy, before printing.

The Archbishop personally reviewed few works, but in 1593, someone got him to personally approve *Venus and Adonis*. The Archbishop had a running battle with the Puritans who defied the licensing laws. In 1599, the Archbishop confiscated and burned thousands of pamphlets and books considered seditious / heretical.

Printing was monopolized by the Stationers' Company (an organization incorporated in 1557 by printers and publishers). The Stationers' Company had sole printing rights in the Kingdom (except for the Oxford and Cambridge University presses) and was empowered to search and seize any book printed in violation of the licensing laws. The Privy Council (Elizabeth's high ranking nobles who acted as her staff) was the supreme executive and judicial body of the state. Lord Hunston, the Lord Chamberlain, sat on the Privy Council. These men controlled all plays. They suppressed any suggestion of treason or heresy.

A list of actors and their affiliations follows:

ELIZABETHAN ACTORS – part 1

ACTOR	CM	KM	SM	AM	PM	other
Alleyn, Edward (1566-1626)	-	-	-	X	-	WoM
Alleyn, John (1557-1596)				X		
Armin, Robert (1568-1615)	-	X	-	-	-	
Benfield, Robert (?-1649)	-	X	-	-	-	CQ
Bird, William (?-1624)	-	-	X	-	X	WoM
Bryan, George (1586-1613)	X	-	X	-	-	LM
Burbage, James (1530-1597)	-	-	-	-	-	LM
*Burbage, Richard (1567-1619)	X	X	X	-	-
*Condell, Henry (?-1627)	X	X	-	-	-
Cowley, Richard (?-1619)	X	X	X	-	-
Ecclestone, William (?-1625+)	-	X	-	-	-	LE
Fletcher, Lawrence (?-1608)	-	?	-	-	-
Goughe, Robert (?-1624)	-	X	X	-	-
*** Heminges, John** (?-1630)	-	X	X	-	-	QM
*** Kempe, Will** (?-1603+)	X	-	X	-	-	LM, WoM
Lowin, John (1576-1653)	-	X	-	-	-	LM, WoM
Ostler, Will (?-1614)	-	X	-	-	-	CC
Phillips, Augustine (?-1605)	X	X	X	-	-
*** Pope, Thomas** (?-1604)	X	-	X	-	-
Robinson, Richard (?-1648)	-	-	X	-	-	CC,CB
*Shaksper, William (1564-1616)	X	X	-	-	-
Singer, John (1583-1609)	-	-	-	-	X	QM
Sly, William (?-1608)	X	X	X			
Tarleton, Richard (?-1588)	-	-	-	-	-	QM, LM

NOTES: *=Sharer Globe Theater, BOLD=Original Chamberlain's Men, **CM**=Chamberlain's Men, **KM**=King's Men, **SM**=Strange's Men, **AM**=Admiral's Men, **PM**=Pembroke's Men, **WoM**= Worcester's Men, **CQ**=Children of Queen's, **LM**=Leicester's Men, **QM**= Queen's Men, **LE**=Lady Elizabeth's Men, **CC**=Children of the Chapel, **CB**=Children of Blackfriar's.

13a. Elizabethan Actors – part 1.

ELIZABETHAN ACTORS – part 2

ACTOR	CM	KM	SM	AM	PM	Other
Adams, John (Sussex and Warwick's Men)	-	-	-			QM
Alleyn, Richard	-	-	-	X	-	
Attewell, George	-	-	-	X	-	WoM
Beeston, Christopher (?-1638)	X	-	-	-	-	WoM
Bentley, John	-	-	-	-	-	QM
Bird, William (?-1624)	-	-	-	X	X	
Cooke, Alexander (?-1614)	-	X	-	-	-	
Cooke, Leonall	-	-	-	-	-	QM
Downton, Thomas (?-1625)	-	-	X		X	
Dutton, John	-	-	-	-	-	QM, OM
Dutton, Laurence	-	-	-	-	-	OM
Garland, John	-	-	-	-	-	QM
Holland, John	X	-	-	-	X	
Hunt, Thomas	-	-	-	X	-	
Jeffes, Humphrey	-	-	-	-	X	
Johnson, William	-	-	-	-	-	LM
Jones, August	-	-	-	X	X	
Jones, Richard	-	-	-	X	-	WoM
Juby, Edward	-	-	-	X	-	
Laneham, John	-	-	-	-	-	LM, QM
Ledbetter, Richard	-	-	-	X	-	
Miles, Thobye	-	-	-	-	-	QM
Perkyn, John	-	-	-	-	-	LM
Sincler, John	X	-	X	-	X	
Slater, Martin		-	-	X	-	
Spencer, Gabriel (?-1598)	X	-	-	X	-	
Towne, John	-	-	-	-	-	QM
Towne, Thomas	-	-	-	X	-	
Tunstall, James	-	-	-	X	-	
Wilson, Robert (?-1600)	-	-	-	-	-	LM,QM

NOTES:
CM=Chamberlain's Men, **KM**=King's Men, **SM**=Strange's Men,
AM=Admiral's Men, **PM**=Pembroke's Men, **OM**=Oxford's Men,
WoM=Worcester's Men, **LM**=Leicester's Men, **QM**=Queen's Men.

13b. Elizabethan Actors – part 2.

Isn't it amazing that with all the actors (and companies) tracked by scholars from various records, there is no listing for Shaksper, prior to the Chamberlain's Men? This is discussed later.

Gary Taylor, in his Introduction to *Reinventing Shakepeare*, describes the Elizabethan actor's life as,

> ...expected to perform in six different plays on six consecutive days. Many times he would rehearse one play in the morning and perform another in the afternoon. On most days he probably played more than one character; Elizabethan actors doubled, trebled, quadrupled roles, their versatility helping to hold down costs.

This was done at subsistence wages (for most actors).

14. Richard Burbage and Edward Alleyn

Andrew Gurr, in *The Shakespearean Stage: 1574-1642*, comments on playwrights of the period and their pay which was poorer than the actors:

Much the largest body of playwriting in the Shakespearean period was hack-work. In the commercial conditions of the time, when all that was asked of the playwrights was to supply the entertainment industry, it could hardly have been anything else. What has survived into this century is probably not a large proportion of the output, though it is likely to include most of the cream. Certainly what is read today is only the cream, and being so it can mislead us about the rest.

The grammar schools set up in the sixteenth century were producing scholars for whom there was no work. The theatre's appetite for plays was the most obvious source of income for such men, talented dramatists or not. And although the demand for plays was great, the number of hack-writers able to supply them was greater still. So it was a buyer's market for plays. Playwrights were the servants of the players, in economic servitude to them. The Cambridge scholars who wrote the Parnassus plays said so from the safety of their university (*2 Return from Parnassus*):

And must the basest trade yeeld us reliefe?
Must we be practis'd to those leaden spouts,
That nought downe vent but what they do receive?
[iv.iv]

There was more money in playing than in play-writing:

With mouthing words that better wits have framed,
They purchase lands, and now Esquiers are made.
[v.i.]

Quite a picture; not in keeping with the artistry of Shake-speare if he was only a hard working actor from Stratford, merely writing plays as a side-line. Also, the land purchasing Esquiers (like Edward Alleyn) were few and far above the average poor actor. Many actors got their start in the children's / boys' companies. These actors received excellent training. The boys' companies were received with favor at Court by the Queen and were often preferred to the less disciplined adult companies. The boys' companies also performed in private theaters. Ben Jonson's *Poetaster* was premiered by the Children of Blackfriar's in 1601; Dekker's and Marston's *Satiro-Matrix* by the Children of Paul's.

Queen Elizabeth's reign began in 1558. She was always interested in music, dancing, spectacle, lavish clothes and Court performances of plays. She was notoriously tight with money, except for her entertainment. Sanitation (like in all of London) was poor in the Queen's palace at Whitehall. When things got unbearably dirty and perfume could not cover up the stench any longer, the palace would be vacated for cleaning purposes.

At these times, Elizabeth would go on 'progresses;' that is, state trips to visit her nobles, where she would pass on to her host the costs of lavishly entertaining and amusing the Queen. These were not puny endeavors, since often 400 carts, 2400 horses and an army of sycophants participated.

Some of the progresses included memorable entertainment. In 1575, the Earl of Leicester presented grand entertainment with cannons and trumpets at Kenilworth. In 1591, Lord Anthony Montagu built an artificial lake and staged a water pageant for the Queen. Others tried to outdo Montagu. Many a noble lived to economically regret his invitation to the Queen. Theobald's, William Cecil's country home, was a favorite of the Queen. She often visited there. In 1572, she visited Havering-in-the-Bowrie, an estate with a 1,000 acre park, owned by the 17th Earl of Oxford, Edward de Vere.

Elizabeth and her English countrymen had multi-faceted tastes. All levels of society enjoyed brutal savagery, the beauty of nature, the heights of poetry, artistic word play, and everything in between. Bull-baiting, bear-baiting, fencing match-es, prize fighting (including female matches), hunt-ing with birds-of-prey / dogs, etc., all had advocates.

15. Cockfighting Arena.

Figure 17 shows Elizabeth hunting. Popular *Titus Andronicus* and *The Spanish Tragedy* were bathed in blood, gore and mayhem, as well as poetry.

Theater, music, dance, sports and entertainment were avid pursuits of the Tudor aristocracy. While the Tudor red rose of Lancaster had triumphed over the white rose of York since 1485 (when Elizabeth's ancestors had won the throne), all was not rosy in Elizabeth's merry olde England.

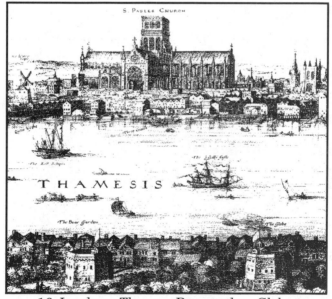

16. London – Thames, Beargarden, Globe.

Points to ponder:

1. With so many actor company affiliations documented, why is Shaksper's affiliation during 1585-93 a blank?

2. Could Will Shaksper, the trainee actor (struggling to support himself between 1585-93), prolifically write plays as a side line?

3. UNMERRY OLDE ENGLAND

When Queen Elizabeth's reign began in 1558, she inherited a poor nation with a depleted treasury; a country factionalized by religious strife; a weak country eyed by powerful Spain and France for domination.

17. Queen Elizabeth hunting.

Elizabethan England was a class-consciously feudal, male-dominated society; a country suffering the ills of widespread poverty, recurring plagues, lack of education, and revolt against the Crown.

The positive changes occurring in Elizabeth's long reign (until 1603) are a testament to her vision, iron-willed determination and careful selection of seasoned, canny politicos such as William Cecil (Lord Burghley), her first minister.

The population of Elizabethan London was approximately 200,000 people. Illiteracy was high. Seventy percent of all English people could neither read nor write. There were no public libraries. There were few private book collections in excess of two thousand items. Continental style, architecture and imports were imitated by the aristocracy, but the spreading European Renaissance (starting in fourteenth century Italy) had not appreciably made its mark across the English Channel.

The first widely used English bible was a product of the fifteen hundreds. This popular 'Geneva' Bible or 'Breetches' Bible was published in 1560, with many subsequent reprints. The *King James Bible* (a project begun in 1604) was first published in 1611. The first English dictionary by Robert Cawdry, *A Table Alphabeticall of Hard Wordes*, also appeared in 1604. Elizabethan spelling was phonetic and erratic. People spelled their words the way they heard them. One had no problem in using variant spellings of a word (on the same page).

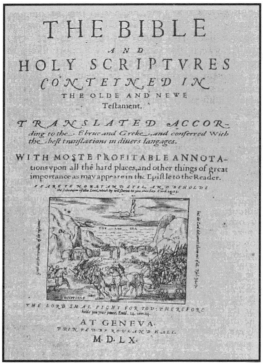

18. The 'Geneva' Bible — Title page.

During Elizabeth's reign, she strongly supported the growth and improvement of grammar schools throughout England. Colleges such as Oxford and Cambridge, which were largely religiously oriented, became more secular in their expanded offerings.

Elizabeth's England became more powerful and cohesive during her reign. Elizabeth contributed by not marrying (precluding a foreign male King), encouraging her cult as 'Virgin Queen,' practicing tight-fisted economic restraint, employing a strong secret service (headed by John Walsingham), and encouraging religious tolerance. While Elizabeth's protestant Church of England was the official religion, a large number of her nobles secretly practised the old religion (Catholicism). The Puritans strongly disagreed with the Church of England's practices. Plots by Catholic nobles to regain the throne and others to topple the throne were always in the making. Mary, Queen of Scots and the Duke of Norfolk are examples of those Elizabeth tried for treason and publicly beheaded.

During Elizabeth's reign (until after 1600 when prices escalated), an artisan or schoolmaster earned about £15/year (about six shillings/week).
The cost of attending a theater performance was one pence (penny). Half of a worker's pay was spent for food. A Tudor soldier received a food allowance of six pence/day, which bought:

> 24 oz. of wheat bread – one pence
> 2/3 of a gallon of beer – one pence
> 2 pounds of beef / mutton (cod / herring) – 2 pence
> 1/2 a pound of butter – one pence
> 1 pound of cheese – one pence
>
> (One pound (£) = 20 shillings = 240 pence = 250+
> 1990's dollars)

Not exactly a nutritionist's idea of a balanced diet! At the other end of the spectrum, nobles and prosperous merchants had incomes of £2000-3000/year. An English middle class of 50,000 people had incomes of £40-500 a year. On stage and in life, the color and style of one's clothes indicated one's class. For example, 'scarlet' was the color of nobility and court officials, while 'blue' was the color used by merchants. It's interesting that a person could afford to attend the theater for the price of a loaf of bread; that is roughly the equivalent to renting a video today.

19. A Plague Doctor.

How did this all affect the theater?

When outbreaks of disease became severe, the theaters closed, such as in 1593. Also, in 1597, all the London theaters were closed when Pembroke's Men presented *Isle of Dogs* by Ben Jonson and Thomas Nashe. The play, an explosive political satire, was suppressed and all copies were tracked down and destroyed. Closing of the theaters forced a Chamberlain's Men tour of the provinces in 1597.

The Puritans were anti-theater and had adherents such as Lord Burghley (a Puritan) in high places. The London civic authorities allowed no theaters to be built inside the London city limits. Puritan attacks on theater cited the stage as being "...a principal source of moral corruption and the habitat of cutpurses and prostitutes."

The Crown believed that theater had strong potential propaganda value, hence encouraged the many history plays of the period (including Shake-speare's) which presented a strong Lancastrian 'spin' on events.

Playwrights cloaked reference to the powerful or despised in many subtle and unsubtle ways. 'Code names,' puns and word play of various types shrouded comment on objects of satire and jest.

The theater was one of the few places in which all strata of Elizabethan society could 'mix.' For this society, theater offered an unbuttoned (within the rules of subterfuge) look at the world, history and English life. On this glorious stage, Shake-spere's words and plays came to life.

So, *Who Were Shake-speare?*

Point to ponder:

1. In a time without a dictionary, how did Shake-speare develop a 30,000 word vocabulary (largest of possibly any playwright)? Perhaps it took Shaksper, de Vere and de Vere's library?

4. THE DYNAMIC DUO

Now, on to the co-writers who used the pen name William Shake-speare! The pseudonym, if looked at as two parts, represents the co-authors. 'William' stands for Will Shaksper from Stratford-upon-Avon. 'Shake-speare' stands for the 'spear-shaker,' Edward de Vere, the 17th Earl of Oxford.

Edward de Vere, the senior partner-mentor-poet was fourteen years older than Shaksper. His shield bore a standing lion shaking a spear. Gabriel Harvey, eulogizing Court figures in Queen Elizabeth's presence (1578), describes Edward as one whose "countenance shakes spears" and praised him as a prolific poet.

20. Lion shaking Spear – Edward de Vere's shield.

Shaksper may have heard of de Vere as early as 1583, when Oxford's Men (touring) played Stratford-upon-Avon. Shaksper was nineteen at the time and a recent father.

WILLIAM

Will Shaksper

21. Will Shaksper

The Young Turk from Stratford-upon-Avon

THEATRICALLY: 'Artistic Director,' actor, theater house-holder (part-owner sharer) and acting company sharer.

LIFE: Shaksper, when he was 18, hastily married a 26 year old, who bore a child within six months. He was father of three (including twins). Shaksper left his wife and family in Stratford (probably with his parents) during his long London residences. He bought property, loaned money (usury), invested venture capital, sued people and testified in court. Shaksper may have suffered memory loss and illness in his later years.

SHAKE-SPEARE

Edward de Vere, 17th Earl of Oxford

22. Edward de Vere, 17th Earl of Oxford

The Spear-Shaking Poet

THEATRICALLY: Company patron, writer, printing patron, theater lessee, and employer of writer-secretaries.

LIFE: De Vere's parents died early. As a Royal Ward, he received Cambridge and Oxford degrees. When he was 20, he married Anne, Lord Burghley's daugther. They had three living children (girls). Edward recognized his illegitimate son Edward (by Anne Vavasor). Later as a widower, he married Bess Trentham. They had one son (Henry). De Vere was a musician, sportsman, courtier and favorite of QE. He was well-traveled, well-read, a book lover and fashion plate. He dissipated his fortune on wine, women, song, theater, etc.

SHAKSPER - to 1585

Shaksper was born in Stratford-upon-Avon in 1564, grew up and received a basic education. At eighteen, he married a twenty-six year old woman (Anne) and had his first child, Susanna, within six months. In the next two years his last children (twins Judith and Hamnet) were born in Stratford (Feb. 1585). Sometime after the twins were born, Shaksper left for London. Wife and family stayed behind in Stratford (presumably with his parents) and apparently never joined Will in London. Did he support them? In 1585, Will was twenty-one and Anne twenty-nine years old.

Early biography, such as obtained from Aubrey, Rowe, Dowdell and Betterton indicates that Shaksper was removed from school to become an apprentice. Aubrey's version follows:

> ...his father was a butcher, and I have been told heretofore by some of his neighbors that, when he was a boy, he exercized his father's trade; but when he killed a calf, he would do it in high style, and make a speech.

Other early insights were:

> 1. That Shaksper left Stratford on some trouble (deer poaching).

> 2. The family did not attend church. Stratford authorities (fearing Catholic plots), listed among other non-church-goers, John Shaksper with the notation, "come not to churche for fear of processe of debte."

3. Will Shaksper was a wit. Mr. Ward, Vicar of Stratford was quoted (in the mid 1600s) as saying, "Mr. Shakspere was a natural wit, without any art at all." Ward also referred to Shaksper's still living daughter and grandaughter in his diary. Susanna Shaksper Hall's tombstone notes that she was like her father, "witty above her sex."

The relationship between Will and Anne Hathaway Shaksper after 1585, was problematical. Will came from a large family, being the third of eight children. Large families were common in Elizabethan times. Will and Anne had no additional children. Was Anne unable to have more children, had they ceased being bedfellows, had Will taken off for London semi-permanently (for over twenty years), or some combination of these?

Surely Will treated Anne (who survived him by nine years) badly in his *Last Will and Testament*. Will left Anne nothing of his ample estate, but "the second best bed." This forced Anne to live at the sufferance of daughter Susanna in the family home bequeathed to Susanna. In any event, Will Shaksper had a failing relationship with Anne in 1585, and sometime after left to follow his star to London.

DE VERE to 1585

Edward de Vere, 35 years old in 1585, was born in 1550 at the ancestral home of the Earls of Oxford, Castle Hedingham. His wealthy family was among the highest ranking English nobility. The de Veres dated back to before William the Conqueror (who married a de Vere). The following biographical information briefly covers Edward de Vere's life through 1585:

1550 **4/22.** Born to parents John de Vere,16th Earl of Oxford, and Margaret Golding de Vere.

1559 Matriculates at Cambridge after years of private tutoring with Arthur Golding (uncle), Thomas Smith and Lord John.

1561 Queen Elizabeth's four day visit to Castle Hedingham includes revels by Lord John's players.

1562 **Sept.** Lord John dies and Edward becomes 17th Earl. Rumor is that John was poisoned, possibly by the Earl of Leicester who acquired many Oxford lands.

Mother quickly remarries Charles Tyrell who had been employed by Edward's father.

Edward becomes a Royal Ward of William Cecil. He resides with, and is educated by Cecil.

1564 **May.** Printing of Arthur Golding's *The histories of Trogus Pompeius*, dedicated to Edward.

Aug. Receives degree from Cambridge University.

1566 Befriends Gabriel Harvey at Cambridge. Receives M.A. at Oxford University.

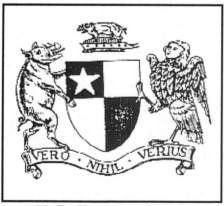

23. De Vere coat of arms.

1567 Printing of Arthur Golding's trans. of Ovid's
Metamorphoses uncharacteristic of Golding.
Partially E.O.?
Admitted Gray's Inn to study law(?)
Kills guardian's (Cecil's) under-cook in swordplay.

1569 Printing of Thomas Underdowne's *Aethiopian
Historie* with dedication to Edward Oxford.
Among the many books Edward purchases is a
'Geneva' Bible. This bible, bearing Edward's
arms, is at the Folger Library (since 1924) and
contains extensive marginalia / underlinings.

1570 Enlists in Earl of Sussex campaign in Scotland.
Distinguished Sussex supports his own acting
company, and is Lord Chamberlain (1572-
1583). Sussex is his strong supporter in Court.
Corresponds with teacher, scientist Dr. John Dee.

24. Tilting in the sixteenth century.

1571 Victor in Queen's Westminster tournament.
Reported as a leading courtier.

Considers helping in the escape of his cousin the
Duke of Norfolk.

Dec. Wed to Anne Cecil, daughter of guardian
William Cecil, newly created Lord Burghley.

1572   Edward writes a Latin preface to Clarke's
Latin translation of *Il Cortegiano*.

Unsuccessfully pleads for Norfolk's life.

Aug. Takes leading part in entertainment at
Warwick Castle.

1573   Printing of Arthur Golding's *Calvin's Version of
the Psalms of David,* dedicated to Edward.

Maintains two apartments at the Savoy, a
bohemian artist mecca.

Printing of Twyne's *Breviary of Britain,* dedicated
to Edward.

Sponsors printing and writes preface to Beding-
field's translation of *Cardanus Comfort.*

1574   Joins QE on a visit to Archbishop of Canterbury.

Visits continent without Queen's permission and
is brought back.

1575   **Jan.** Sets out with retinue of eight on authorized
visit to the continent.

Mar.-Apr. In Paris, then visits Sturmius (a
leading scholar) in Strasbourg.

May-Dec. In Italy, from Venice to Genoa.

Challenges jousters in Palermo.

Sep. Learns his daughter Elizabeth, who is sup-
posedly born in July, is christened in Sept.

1576   **Mar.** Is back in France.

Apr. Suspects his child Elizabeth is not his. Is
robbed by pirates on his hasty return to
England. Begins five year separation from wife
Anne, during which time he selectively self-
exiles himself from Court.

E.O. poems in *Paradyse of Daintie Devices.*

Sells five estates.

1577   **May.** Invests in Frobisher's New World voyage.

Printing of Brooke's *The Staff of Christian Faith,*
dedicated to Edward.

John Lyly, later his secretary, living at Savoy (on

Edward's tab?).

Sells three estates.

1578 **May.** Invests in Frobisher's second voyage.

July. Gabriel Harvey eulogises courtiers in Queen's presence. Oxford is praised as prolific poet whose "countenance shakes spears."

Is head of *Euphuist* cultural movement.

Sells two estates.

Queen grants Edward the Manor of Rysing.

1579 **July.** Lyly, now his secretary, registers *Euphues and His England,* dedicated to Edward.

Printing of Anthony Munday's *Mirror of Mutabilitie,* dedicated to Edward.

Sep. Quarrels with Philip Sidney on tennis court.

Sells five estates.

1580 "a pleasant conceit . . . by de Vere" is performed at Court (an early version of *Twelfth Night?*).

Printing of Munday's *Zelauto,* dedicated to Edward, and calling Edward "*Euphues.*"

Takes over Earl of Warwick's acting company.

Entertains crowd in Royal Progress to Plymouth.

Denounces Catholics – Howard (cousin), Arundel and Southwell; with whom he previously practised the old religion (Catholicism) until treason against the Queen surfaced.

Sells thirteen estates.

1581 Wins prize in Queen's tournament.

Mar. Anne Vavasor, QE's Maid of honor, bears his natural son, Edward Vere. Edward, Anne and the babe are imprisoned in the 'Tower.'

Edward out under house arrest six weeks later.

Oct. Purchases ship, *Edward Bonaventure?*

Dec. Resumes living with wife, Anne.

1582 **Mar.** Is wounded by Thomas Knyvet (Vavasor's uncle) in an ongoing vendetta.

Printing of Watson's *Hekatompathia,* dedicated to Edward. Is Edward also a contributor?

Sells four estates.

1583 His newly born son Henry dies and is buried.

Spring. Acquires sub-lease Blackfriar's Theatre and transfers to Lyly.

John Dutton transfers from Oxford's Men to newly formed Queen's Men.

Under Edward's patronage, *Agamemnon and Ulysses* performed at Court. Was this an early version of *Troilus and Cressida?*

1583-84 His acting company tours (including Stratford).

1584 Apr. Daughter Bridget born to the de Veres.

Spring. Lyly's *Campaspe* performed at Court by Oxford's company (co-written Edward?).

Takes over Earl of Worcester's Company.

Robert Greene's *Greene's Card of Fancy* printed with a dedication to Edward.

Acquires fancy London home, 'Fisher's Folly.'

Sootherne's *Pandora* printed containing wife Anne's 'Epitaphs' and ode praising Edward.

8/29. To Flanders to command Queen's cavalry.

9/21. On return to England captured by pirates. Father-in-law Lord Burghley protests to Dutch and he is released.

11/17. Wins in Queen's tournament.

Dec. *The History of Agamemnon and Ulysses* performed at Court by Oxford's Boys. Is this an early version of *Troilus and Cressida?*

1585 Challenged to duel Vavasor's brother.

By 1585, Edward de Vere had experienced family losses, education, travel, a rocky marriage, being a favorite of Queen Elizabeth, winning tournaments, battle and life experience. He had dissipated (or lost through the connivance of others) much of his great fortune. He had become a well known, dedicated and discerning patron of the arts (of writers and acting companies particularly), written and published poetry (at his expense) and was noted for his poetry and Court playwriting / presentations.

COLLABORATORS AHOY

In subsequent chapters we provide background, detail, evidence and corroboration to show that:

> Ultimately, de Vere and Shaksper became the 'Dynamic Duo,' collaborators on the Shake-speare plays. De Vere was mentor and subsidizer of Shaksper. De Vere enhanced the collaboration by exploiting his poetic vision, contacts, library, education, travel experience and stable of writer-secretaries.

Shaksper the actor, 'Artistic Director,' the inside man at the Chamberlain's-King's Men and 'Globe' contributed his youthful vigor, day-to-day theatrical know how, deep observation of human character, depictions of workers / tradesmen and rollicking low comedic talent to the collaboration. The latrine humor about 'jakes,' bawdy / fat jokes, etc., echo the mindset of Shaksper's tombstone doggerel:

> Good friend, for Jesus' sake forbear
> To dig the dust enclosed here.
> Blest be the man that spares these stones,
> And curst be he that moves my bones.

Shaksper and de Vere left a clear and voluminous trail of their 'fingerprints and footprints' in the Shake-speare plays. Viewing the plays as a collaborative effort over a period from well before 1590 (beginning with de Vere's solo forays in the 1570s), to Shaksper's death in 1616, changes the Shake-speare picture considerably.

Procrustean dating of the Shake-speare plays becomes unnecessary. Shaksper's birthdate in 1565, and his limited time to gain playwriting experience by 1589 (when he was 24 years old), causes dating problems for Stratfordians. As a result Stratfordian scholars tend to date Shake-speare plays later than evidence suggests, compress the time frame in which the body of plays were written and gloss over the maturity displayed in the *Bard's* 'first efforts.'

Supporters of de Vere's as the sole author Shake-speare (Oxfordians) have been accused of early dating the late plays to match de Vere's death in 1604.

The potpourri of wide ranging styles in the Shake-speare plays, particularly older styles out of favor, becomes more comprehensible in a de Vere-Shaksper collaboration. Consider the ponderously poetic fourteen liners in the *Comedy of Errors* (an early play). The fourteen liners hark back to the poulter's meter of the poem attributed to Arthur Brooke, *Romeus and Juliet* (1563) and de Vere early poetry.

Consider the Euphuist (flowery and exaggeratedly stylized language) influences and correlations in the plays, *A Comedy of Errors, Two Gentlemen of Verona, The Taming of the Shrew, A Midsummer Night's Dream, Much Ado About Nothing, As You*

Like It and *Twelfth Night*. Interestingly, John Lyly, the father of Euphuism, during the Euphuist heyday (early 1580's) was de Vere's secretary and paymaster for Oxford's Boys and Oxford's Men, etc.

SHAKSPER's HANDPRINTS

The hand of Shaksper shows in describing the character of the constable Dogberry (his father was a constable), etc. Kate, the 'shrew' may have been modeled after an unrepentant wife, Anne and Shylock the 'moneylender' after personal experience as a usurer. An interesting book, *Shakespeare's Professional Skills* by Neville Coghill, makes the case for Shake-speare's intimately superior knowledge of actors, theater and the stage (gained firstand through years of labor). Coghill states,

> ...among his plays, is the continual exercise of craftmanlike understanding in his art, such as I think cannot be matched (save for flashes here and there) in the work of his contemporaries. He always seemed to know how to use, or to extend (by a kind of dramatic strategy) the resources at the disposal of a playwright.

Hamlet's speech to the actors comes right from the 'Artistic Director' of the Chamberlain's Men:

Enter HAMLET and Players.

Hamlet: Speak the speech, I pray you, as I pronounced it to you,
    trippingly on the tongue :
      but if you mouth it, as many of your players do,
        I had as lief the town-crier spoke my lines.
      Nor do not saw the air too much with your hand, thus,

but use all gently ;

for in the very torrent, tempest, and, as I may say,
the whirlwind of passion, you must, you must acquire
and beget a temperance that may give it smoothness.
O, it offends me to the soul to hear a robustious periwig-pated
fellow tear a passion to tatters, to very rags,
to split the ears of the groundlings, who for the most part are
capable of nothing but inexplicable dumb-shows and noise :
I would have such a fellow whipped for o'erdoing Termagant :
it out-herods Herod : pray you avoid it.

First Player:
I warrant your honor.

Hamlet: Be not too tame neither, but let your own discretion be your tutor :
suit the action to the word, the word to the action ;
with this special observance that you o'ersep not
the modesty of nature :
for any thing so overdone is from the purpose of playing,
whose end, both at the first and now, was and is, to hold,
as 'twere, the mirror up to nature ;
to show virtue her own feature, scorn her own image,
and the very age and body of the time his form and pressure.
Now this overdone, or come tardy off,
though it make the unskilful laugh,
cannot by make the judicious grieve ; the censure of which one
must in your allowance o'erweigh a whole theatre of others.
O, there be players that I have seen play, and heard others praise,
and that highly, not to speak it profanely, that,
neither having the accent of Christians
nor the gait of Christian, pagan, nor man,
have so strutted and bellowed that I have thought some of nature's
journeymen had made men and not made them well,
they imitated humanity so abominably.

First player:
I hope we have reformed that indifferently with us, sir.

Hamlet: O, reform it altogether.
And let those who play your clowns speak no more than is
set down for them ;
for there be of them that will themselves laugh,
to set on some quantity of barren spectators to laugh too ;
though, in the mean time,

some necessary question of the play be then to be considered :
that's villainous,
        and shows a most pitiful ambition in the fool that uses it.
Go, make you ready.

DE VERE's FOOTPRINTS

The authentic Italian settings, Italian names, and love of things 'Italianate' in the Shake-speare plays are a product of de Vere's travel and experience in Padua, Florence, Venice, etc. Plays like *The Merchant of Venice, Taming of the Shrew, Othello*, and *All's Well That End's Well* soak up de Vere's Italian experience.

Caricatures of courtiers and the mighty, people like his opponent at Court, Christopher Hatton (Malvolio) and Lord Burghley required the insider, de Vere. Polonius in *Hamlet* (a caricature of Burghley) utters lines from Lord Burghley's yet unpublished *Certaine Preceptes*. His son-in-law, Edward de Vere is playing again. Hunchbacked Robert Cecil was a model for villainous Richard III.

Autobiographical interjections in *Hamlet* and use of the friend Horatio point to de Vere's footprints again. The first English person christened with the given name Horatio was Horatio Vere, Edward's beloved younger cousin, born in 1563. Withycombe's *Oxford Dictionary of English Christian Names*, includes the following entry for the name Horace (Horatio):

... Its use as a christian name dates from the Renaissance, and seems to have started (as Horatio) [Orazio] in Italy

(cf. Shakespear's *Horatio* in *Hamlet*). The earliest
example noted in England is Sir *Horatio* Vere (1563-
1635), 1st Lord Vere of Tilbury.

More than a third of the Shake-speare plays use
'Italianate' character names, many ending in 'io'
pronounced E-O (like Edward Oxford's initials).
Mercutio (mercurial), Malvolio (malevolent),
Dromio (dromedary for servant), and Romeo are
invented names. Oxford had a field day with the
names in *Taming of the Shrew*; Vincentio,
Petruchio, Gromio, Hortensio, Tranio and Grumio.
Romeo is pronounced as if it were written Romio,
emphasizing the letters E-O (Oxford's initials) The
latin 'eo' (as in Deo) is pronounced 'ay-o.' Romeo is
properly pronounced, Ro-may-o. Edward Oxford is
having his fun.

Oxford caricatured and commented on Court life in
the plays. As a courtier and highly born noble, he
was well able to experience this highly restricted
aspect of English life. His station allowed him to
produce sharply painted portraits of the nobility
without suffering the fate of lesser born playwrights (censorship and/or worse).

Oxford's royal and aristocratic viewpoint (laden
with Lancastrian sympathies) fills the plays. This
is a mirror of his character and class. Oxford and
Shaksper enjoyed a good joke. Fancy word play
would be used by these co-writers to convey humor,
or as an end in itself. What fun they must have had
in selecting / using the pen name William Shake-
speare; William for sweet William the shepherd or

rustic, and Shake-speare for the spear-shaker, Edward de Vere, 17th Earl of Oxford.

In the sixteenth century, de Vere (pronouned 'dc Vair') rhymed with Shake-speare (pronounced 'Shiek-spair'). Oxford, known in court as the 'spear shaker' (for his tournament wins and emblems), was also aware that Pallas Athena, patron godess of Athens / Greek theater, was nick-named *Hasti-vibrans* (spear shaker).

SHAKE-SPEARE's KNOWLEDGE

Shakespeare's flowers, by Jessica Kerr.
Shakespeare's Italian settings and plays, by Murray J. Levith.
Shakespeare's legal acquirements..., by John Lord Campbell.
Shakespeare and the dance, by Alan Brissenden.
English history in Shakespeare's plays, by Beverly Ellison.
Shakespeare and the classics, by J. A. K. Thomson.
World of Shakespeare: animals & monsters, by Alan Dent.
Shakespeare's heraldry, by C. W. Scott-Giles.
Shakespeare's Biblical knowledge and... , by Richmond Noble.
Shakespeare and music, by Edward W. Naylor.
The birds of Shakespeare..., by Grundy Steiner.
Shakespeare and medicine, by Robert Simpson.
Shakespeare's military world, by Paul Jorgenson.
A glossary of Shakespeare's sea and naval terms, including
    gunnery, by Alexander Falconer.
"Courtesy" in Shakespeare, by M. M. Bhattacherje.
Folk-lore of Shakespeare, by Thomas Thiselton-Dyer.
Shakespeare and the arts of design (architecture, sculpture,
    and painting), by Arthur Fairchild.
Astronomy in the poets, by Cumberland Clark.
Shakespeare's economics, by Henry W. Farnam.
Shakespeare and the geography..., by John Gillies.
Shakespeare once a printer and bookman, by William Jaggard.
Shakespeare as a scientist..., by Oliver Ellis.
Shakespeare's Scotland, by James Fergusson.
Espana en Shakespeare, by Pedro Duque.
World of Shakespeare: sports & pastimes, by Alan Dent.
Shakespeare as an angler, by Henry Ellacombe.
Shakespeare an archer, by William Rushton.
    The mediaeval dimension in Shakespeare's plays, by Milward.

---

25. Shake-speare's Knowledge – (as described in books).

Oxford's education and library were a necessary ingredient in producing the body of works previously described as an 'Encyclopedia Elizabetheana.' The previous list presents a small number of the books / subjects written about Shake-speare's knowledge.

Edward Oxford enjoyed the humor of sharing the pen name William Shake-speare. The similarity of the pseudonym to the real name of his protégé, Will Shaksper offered additional advantages. Oxford, because of his title and status could not publicly admit to participating in writing plays. What better way to obscure the de Vere participation, than letting the co-writer (Shaksper) appear to the unknowing world, as sole writer.

Points to ponder:

1. Multiple styles in individual Shake-speare plays expose the collaborative hands.

2. Use of older (out of date) styles such as 'Euphuism,' and ponderous fourteen line verses, harken to earlier days, and the earlier efforts of Edward de Vere.

3. Court insider information, intimate depictions of the powerful and famous, as well as biographical insights into the life of Edward de Vere, expose the Earl of Oxford as a collaborator.

5. SWEET WILLIAM

Will Shaksper, the modestly educated provincial from Stratford, goes to London where he becomes enmeshed in the theatrical life of the town. Then he rises to the position of actor/sharer/artistic director of the Chamberlain's and King's Men. He is also a sharer in the Globe Theatre, is one of the Lessees of the Blackfriar's Theatre, and is co-writer with Edward de Vere of the Shake-speare plays. How did all this happen?

We left Will Shaksper in 1585, when his twins were born; then leaving for London, possibly as early as 1585.

Shaksper did rise to become a sharer (part owner) of the Chamberlain's / King's Men and Globe Theatre. The early trail is non-existent and evidence is sparse, but it is there. To begin with, let's discuss the background of a critical document.

Proponents of persons other than Will Shaksper as the sole writer of the Shake-speare works have claimed that Shaksper:

1. Was illiterate and could not read or write, on the basis of his badly formed signatures and lack of any documentation that Shaksper

attended Stratford Grammar School (or any other school).

2. Came from an illiterate family and had illiterate children, on the basis of his father John signing documents with a cross, etc.

Proponents of Will Shaksper as the sole writer of the Shake-speare works claim that:

1. He had to attend the grammar school because the quality of the Shake-speare works requires education. The proponents tend to paint an inflated picture of the Stratford Grammar School.

2. Point out that John Shaksper (with two others) was responsible for keeping the Stratford books and that it was common practice for officials to use a cross in lieu of their signature.

26. New Place – Shaksper's Stratford home.

In 1635, a petition was brought by three actor sharers in the King's Men to acquire shares in the Globe Theatre and Blackfriar's Theatre from, among others, Cuthbert Burbage, and both Richard Burbage's son and remarried widow.

While acting company shares generally expired on retirement of the actor, theater shares (or housekeeper shares) were property which could be retained by the actor and became part of the actor's estate. In this particular case, Richard Burbage's shares were bequeathed to his son and wife. A petition to acquire the Burbage theater shares was brought before the Lord Chamberlain, Philip Herbert (Lord Montgomery of the *First Folio* of 1623; now 4th Earl of Pembroke). The 'Burbages' prefaced their response to the petition with the following 'Globe' and Blackfriar's Theatre history:

A KEY DOCUMENT - EXCERPT

The father of us, Cuthbert and Richard Burbage, was the first builder of playhowses, and was himself in his younger yeeres a player. The Theater he built with many hundred pounds taken up at interest, – The players that lived in those first times had only the profitts arising from the dores, but now the players receave all the commings in at the dores to themselves and halfe the galleries from the housekeepers. Hee built this house upon leased ground, by which meanes the landlord and hee had a great suite in law, and, by his death, the like troubles fell upon us, his sonnes; wee then bethought us of altering from thence, and at like expense built the Globe, with more summes of money taken up at interest, which lay heavy on us many yeeres, and to ourselves we joyned those deserving men, **Shakspere**, Hemings, Condell, Philips and others, partners in the profittes of that they call the House, but making the leases for twenty-one yeeres hath beene the destruction of ourselves and others, for they dyeing at the expiration of three or four yeeres of their lease, the subsequent yeeres became dissolved to strangers, as by marrying their widdowes, and the like by their children.– Thus Right Honorable, as concerning the Globe, where wee ourselves are but lessees. Now for the Blackfriar's, that is our inheritance; our father purchased it at extreame rates, and made it into a playhouse with great charge and troble; which after was leased out to one Evans that first sett up the boyes commonly called Queenes Majesties Children of the Chappell. In processe of time, the boyes growing vp to be men, which were Underwood, Field, Ostler, and were taken to strengthen the Kings service; and more to strengthen the service, the boyes dayly wearing out, it was considered that house would bee as fitt for ourselves, and soe purchased the lease remaining from Evans with our money, and placed men players, which were Hemings, Condell **Shakspeare**, &c."

A KEY DOCUMENT – ANALYSIS

Some points to consider about the Burbage statement include:

1. Burbage used 'Shakspere' and 'Shakspeare' the man's true name in the statement, not Shake-speare (with the letter 'e' in the first syllable).

2. The statement that Shaksper was a share-holder in the Globe Theatre in 1599 is corroborated by testimony stating this, given by John Heminges and Henry Condell in 1619.

3. Burbage's statement was presented to the 4th Earl of Pembroke (fomerly Earl of Montgomery), one of the two brothers, to whom Shake-speare's *First Folio* of 1623 is dedicated.

27. The Original Shaksper Monument.

Some conclusions:

1. Will Shaksper was a shareholder (part owner) in the Globe Theatre in 1599.

2. Will Shaksper was a shareholder in the Chamberlain's Men in 1599, or he could not have become, with other Company shareholders (Hemmings, Condell, Philips, etc.), a Globe Theatre shareholder.

3. Will Shaksper could read and write. If illiterate, he could not become a Chamberlain's Men / Globe Theatre shareholder. How could the members of a leading acting company, working continuously with new handwritten playscripts, etc., allow an illiterate to become a part owner of their company and theatre?

4. Will, being a Chamberlain's Men / Globe Theatre shareholder, could read and write. Therefore, he must have received some education, most likely at Stratford Grammar School.

5. The above lend credence to support the questioned December, 1594 entry in QE's Accounts of the Treasurer of the Chamber. The entry records a payment of £20 to "Will Kempe Will Shakespeare & Richard Burbage servants of the Lord Chamb[er]lain..." This acknowledges Shaksper (the Chamberlain's servant) as an important member of the Company (shareholder) in 1594. The account was

prepared posthumously (to the death of William
Heneage, the Treasurer of the Chamber), by his
widow (Mary Browne, Former Countess of
Southampton and daughter of Anthony,
Viscount Montagu). Though the entry lacks
accuracy in other matters, there would seem no
reason that the listed Chamberlain's Men would
be incorrect.

6. With all of the above (items one through six),
the following for Shaksper makes sense:

    a. Receiving cloth in 1604 for the Royal
Progress through London.

28. Stratford Grammar School.

    b. King's Men actor, Augustine Phillipps
(died in 1605) wills with a small bequest

to fellow actors, including Shaksper.

c. In 1607, being one of seven who leased the Blackfriar's Theatre.

d. In 1613, bought a house for investment in Blackfriar's near the theater.

Shaksper's life between 1585-1593 is discussed further in chapters six *(1585-1593, Mystery Years)*, and chapter nine *(Chamberlain and Globe)*. For now, suffice to say that between 1585-1603, Shaksper went to London, and after years of apprenticeship joined the Chamberlain's Men during the golden years (1594-1603) as the distinguished artistic director, resident co-playwright and sometime actor.

Shaksper's activity after 1603 is described in the following list:

1604-16 In Stratford leases, named as owner of adjacent property.
1604   **March**. Listed with those to receive cloth for King's London procession.
            July. Sues Philip Rogers, Stratford apothecary.
1605   **May**. Augustine Phillips, King's Men actor, makes will in which he bequeaths £5 "unto and amongst the hired men of the Company", among whom Shaksper is listed.
            July. Purchases 1/4 Stratford corn and hay tithes for £440.
1607   6/5. Daughter Susanna weds Dr. John Hall.
1608   2/11. Grandaughter Elizabeth Hall born.
            8/9. Becomes one of the lessees of the Blackfriar's Theatre.
            9/7. Mother is buried in Stratford.
1608-9 Sues John Addercombe of Stratford to recover a debt.
1610   Involved legal action on *New Place* and 20 acres of land.
1611   Added to list of contributers to Stratford highway fund.

1612 London: lodged with Huguenot wigmaker, Mountjoy. Signs deposition as "of Stratford upon Avon."
1613 John Combe of Stratford dies, and leaves him £5.
Blackfriar's district, London: buys house as "of Stratford upon Avon" and leases back to seller.
1614 Collects from Stratford town 2 quarts wine he served to a preacher.
Thomas Greene document shows Shaksper owns 127 acres of land.
Shaksper and son-in-law Dr. John Hall in London on business, related to Stratford tithes.
Fall. Involved in enclosing Stratford common lands.
1615 Shaksper is a party to a suit related to Blackfriar's Theatre.
1616 **2/10**. Daughter Judith marries Thomas Quiney without license, and they are excommunicated.
3/15. Makes last will and testament.
4/25. Listed in the burial register of Trinity Church.
1622 Monument erected in Trinity Church.

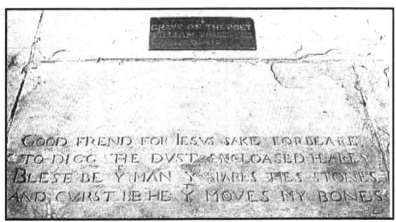

29. Shaksper's Grave.

What emerges is that after 1604 (the year of Oxford's death), Shaksper gradually reduced his London activity until he retired exclusively to Stratford.

Two Shaksper epitaphs collected around 1650 by Nicolas Burgh, a Windsor resident, offer us some insight. The epitaphs are contained in Bodleian Ashmolean MS 38. One is for John Combe, a Stratford resident and friend of Shaksper, the other for Ben Jonson. Before presenting the Burgh epitaphs, let's look at a corroborating Combe epitaph (written while Combe, a notorious usurer was alive), as presented by biographer Rowe:

> "(Combe's reaction) the sharpness of the satire . . . stung the man so severely that he never forgave it."

> Ten is the hundred lies here engraved;
> 'Tis a hundred to ten his soul is not saved.
> If any man ask, "Who lies in this tomb?"
> "Oh! ho!" quoth the devil, " 'tis my John-a Combe."

Now Burgh's 'Shaksper' epitaphs:

> On John Combe a Covetous rich man Mr. Wm.
> **Shakspear** wright that att his request while hee was yett living for his Epitaphe
>> Who Lies In this Tombe
>> Hough; quoth the Devil, Tis my Sonn
>> John A Combe.

> finis

> but being dead, and making the poor his heiers he after wrightes this for his Epitaph

>> How ere he lived judge not
>> John Combe will never be forgott
>> While poor, hath Memmorye, for he did gather
>> To make the poor his Issue; he their father
>> As record of his tilth and seede
>> Did Crowne him In his Latter deede.
>> finis W : **Shak**.

Interesting! Described and signed Shaksper. This sounds like Shaksper's tombstone dogerrel. Also, it corresponds to the fact that Combe left £1000 to the poor. The Jonson epitaph reads:

> Mr. Ben Jonson and Mr. Wm. **Shake-speare** Being Merrye att a Tavern, Mr. Jonson haveing begune this for his Epitaph
> Here lies Ben Jonson that was once one he gives ytt to Mr **Shakspear** to make up who presently wrightes
>
> Who while he liv'de was a slow thinge
> and now being dead is Nothinge.
> finis

E. K. Chambers in *William Shakespeare*, 1930, says that the Jonson verse "...may have had its source in Jonson's reputation as a slow writer, a circumstance he was frequently twitted for by his contemporaries."

My thought is that this may be another example of the humor of Will Shaksper, the rough rustic, co-writer of the dynamic duo.

PROOF SHAKE-SPEARE WAS A PEN NAME?

The Jonson verse describes the writers Shakespeare (hyphenated) and Jonson (not hyphenated), then goes on to describe Mr. Shakspear penning an epitaph.

Shaksper, or whoever wrote these verses, distinguishes the writer the world knows as **Shakespeare** from the man **Shaksper** (as he was known to family, neighbors, friends and intimates). Was the distinction merely that they were pronounced and spelled differently?

It was not general knowledge in Elizabethan England that Will Shaksper participated in creating the works of William Shake-speare. William Camden, in his *Annals* for the year 1616, omits Shaksper's death, yet in his *Remaines* praises 'Shakespeare.' In Camden's list of Stratford worthies for 1605, Shaksper's name is missing, though Camden had previously passed on the Shaksper application for a coat of arms. Camden appreciated Shake-speare as a poet and playwright, but did not connect the pen name William Shake-speare with Will Shaksper from Stratford.

The three page, *Last Will and Testament* of Shaksper is very detailed in the nature of bequests and contains interlineations (spur of the moment changes).

The will left the bulk of Shaksper's estate to his daughter, Susanna. He provided in a small way for his daughter, Judith and her issue. Wife, Anne, was left with only the second best bed. Associates Burbage, Condell and Heminges were to receive token amounts to purchase memorial rings.

Small bequests were made to acquaintances. While household items were minutely described, there were no theater shares, books or manuscripts

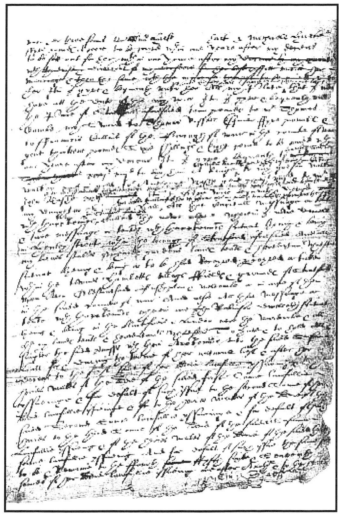

30. Shaksper's '*Will*' – Page two of three.

described. Were there none? Was Shaksper's mind failing?

In all, the will has a haphazard feel about it. There are mispellings of names Shaksper knew well and

his signatures are shaky. Poor health and/or failing memory had taken their toll.

E. K. Chambers has suggested that in 1612,
Shaksper's memory was already failing. He notes
that he was unable to recall circumstances crucial
to the Belott-Mountjoy deposition. Charles Hamilton makes a similar case in his book, *In Search of
Shakespeare.*

This Tragœdie vvas firſt
acted, in the yeere
1603.

By the Kings Maieſties
SERVANTS.

The principall Tragœdians were,

Ric. Burbadge.	Will. Shake-Speare.	
Avg. Philips.	Ioh. Hemings.	
Wil.Slt.	Hen. Condil.	
Ion. Lowin.	Alex. Cooke.	

With the allowance of the Maſter of REVELLS.

31. *Sejanus* cast – Jonson's 1616 edition.

Shaksper's memory lapses would render him
useless as an actor on the stage. In 1616, Ben

Jonson published a collection of his own works. Included was a playlist for *Sejanus* which was first performed in 1603. (See figure 31 on the previous page for *Sejanus* playlist.) Jonson varied the practice of using 'Shake-speare' in print. Jonson, the careful editor, had his fun spelling it SHAKE-SPEARE. Was he hinting at a pen name? Was sly Jonson referring to Shaksper or de Vere in the cast? With the vagaries of Elizabethan play performance (one or two performances akin to a reading of today), Edward de Vere might have occasionally performed a role incognito.

The original Shaksper monument in Stratford was erected sometime before the printing of the *First Folio* in 1623. Dugdale's *Antiquities of Warwickshire* (1656) and the revised edition depicted the original monument, as did Nicolas Rowe in his book, *Life of Shakespeare* (1709). All three show a merchant holding a distended bag of grain, rather than the current pen on a pillow. (See figure 26.) In any event, the monument inscription follows:

IUDICIO PYLIUM, GENIO SOCRATEM, ARTE MARONEM:
TERRA TEGIT, POVLVS MAERET, OLYMPUS HABET.

STAY PASSENGER, WHY GOEST THOV BY SO FAST?
READ IF THOU CANST, WHOM ENVIOVS DEATH HATH PLAST
WITH IN THIS MONVMENT SHAKESPEARE: WITH WHOM,
QUICK NATVRE DIDE: WHOSE NAME DOTH DECK Y TOMBE.
FAR MORE THAN COST: SIEH ALL, YT HE HATH WRITT,
LEAVES LIVING ART, BVT PAGE, TO SERVE HIS WITT.

32. Stratford Monument inscription.

Rather strange. Only the surname 'Shakespeare' with no dates, nothing about writing plays or poems, and not placed on the indicated tomb (since Shaksper's grave was outside the church). The monument was probably produced by non-family, in London, from afar, rather indifferently, as part of the *First Folio* project. Is the vagueness to conceal the co-authorship?

The case for Shaksper preparing his will is made in Charles Hamilton's *In Search of Shakespeare*. Handwritten, holographic wills were fairly common in the seventeenth century. Hamilton presents paleographic evidence that Shaksper (the will preparer) suffered a stroke / poisoning during preparation of the document.

33. Shaksper Monument – current bust.

Will Shaksper spent the greater part of his life in Stratford-upon-Avon and referred to himself (when in London) as from Stratford-upon-Avon. Except for the period Shaksper was in London between 1585-1605, there is little in his life of a literary nature. At Shaksper's death no eulogies were written, nor were there any special theatrical celebrations (in his home town or in London). Posthumous stories about Will Shaksper recount his wit, his deer poaching and his drinking bouts.

Shaksper was born into a lower middle class family of tradesmen, farmers and sometime town officials. In efforts to inflate Will's background one finds the words 'wealthy', 'influential' and 'aristoctratic' in biographies. Such terms are misleading. Will's mother, Mary, was the youngest of eight daughters of farmer Robert Arden of Wilmcote. After Mary's mother died, her farmer father, Robert, remarried a farmer's widow. Mary's line has not been traced further back than her grandfather, Thomas Arden, who initially bought (farmed?) Wilmcote property. Some biographers indicate that Mary's family may have been related to the patrician Ardens of Park Hall. It is likely that Mary never met or knew these people of a vastly different social class. Robert Arden may have been prosperous but could not be considered wealthy by any reasonable Elizabethan standard. Robert Arden had a home, the smallholding he farmed and two additional freeholds. He rented one of these freeholds to Richard Shaksper, Will's paternal grandfather. That is how the two families were acquainted. No one related to Will Shaksper by blood or marriage possesed even a simple knighthood. When Will's father John (who suffered economic reverses in his later years) applied for a knighthood, for the first time, his application was rejected.

Will Shaksper was the most economically successful of his relatives by blood or marriage. He felt
comfortable acquiring material things, protecting
his property / monetary interests legally, and being
patriarch of his dysfunctional family. Shaksper's
talent and latent genius found expression during
his London years when he collaborated with
Edward de Vere and participated in the golden
years of the Chamberlain's Men. Shaksper's part in
the collaboration has since been disproportionately
honored and adulated as the sole creative force
(Shake-speare).

Point to ponder:

1. When is the last time you wrote on a pillow (as
depicted in the currently modified Shaksper monument)?

34. *First Folio* Title Page.

6. 1585-1593 – MYSTERY YEARS

1585 to 1593 is the ultimate mystery period of English theater. This is the time that:

> William Shaksper receives the wide experience and training that allows him to become the seasoned professional, accepted as sharer of the Chamberlain's Men. The mystery is in the details.

> Christopher Marlowe writes all of his own works, collaborates, receives support from an unknown patron, then dies under suspicious circumstances in 1593.

> Thomas Kyd supposedly pens his one 'hit' (very unlike other Kyd works), 'The Spanish Tragedy.' Kyd lives with Chrisopher Marlowe (to Kyd's later regret). Kyd receives support from an unknown patron. The nobleman drops Kyd, when under torture, Kyd incriminates Marlowe for heresy (atheistic and hedonistic tendencies).

> The future Chamberlain's Men founders are all actors in Strange's Men (Lord Derby's

company), and are performing plays which are later ascribed to Shake-speare.

Pembroke's Men are performing plays which are later ascribed to Shake-speare.

Sussex's Men (under sponsorship of the 4th Earl) are performing plays which are later ascribed to Shake-speare. The 3rd Earl of Sussex, a strong supporter of Edward de Vere in Court, was Lord Chamberlain from 1572 to 1583 (when he died).

Oxford's Men and Oxford's Boys are active, performing before the Queen, Court, privately and publicly. They compete on broadsides with the Admiral's Men, Leicester's Men, etc. The Blackfriar's Theatre is sub-leased and used by Oxford.

Prolific Edward de Vere suddenly stills his pen. Maybe not! De Vere has anonymously published poems, presented plays at Court, is patron of two acting companies, writers, and has as secretaries, Lyly and Munday.

The 'University Wits' (Marlowe, Greene, Peele, Nashe and Lodge), Oxford or Cambridge University men, are penning plays for the professional theater in the late 1580s; when taking a break from their major activity, dissolute living.

First, some background on the 1580's. The Queen's Men, organized in 1583, is a dominant acting company until 1588, when Richard Tarleton dies. Leicester's Men (an important London company), is disbanded in 1588 when Robert Dudley, the Earl of Leicester dies. Sussex's Men plays the provinces as do Worcester's Men and Strange's (Derby's) Men. Pembroke's Men is not active until the 1590's.

Oxford's Men and combined Oxford's Boy's / Paul's Boys are leading London acting companies, as the Queen's Men decline after Tarleton's death (1588).

Oxford sub-leases the Blackfriar's Theatre. The largest number of Court appearances in this decade is by Oxford's companies. In fact, the only nobleman (patron) personally involved in London theater is Edward de Vere, 17th Earl of Oxford.

We have noted that Oxford's Men played Stratford-upon-Avon in 1583. Legend has it that poaching a deer from Sir Thomas Lucy of Charlecotte (a local Stratford luminary) was the cause of Will Shaksper leaving for London. This is curious because Lucy had no gaming preserves (but did have a warren) in the Stratford area.

Perhaps the legend was confused. The Warden's and Chamberlain's accounts for the town of Coventry list performances in 1584 of Sir Thomas Lucy's acting company. Sir Thomas apparently did have a provincial company in Stratford that played other towns.

Eva Clark's *Hidden Allusions in Shakespeare's Plays* makes the case for Will Shaksper acting with Lucy's provincial company, and then being 'poached' by Oxford's Men. This is a way Shaksper could have begun associating with Oxford.

The following is from *The English Chronicles* of John Payne Collier, about a soldier's letter to Secretary Walsingham in 1586:

> "every day in the week the players' bills are set up in sundry places in the city," and after mentioning the actors to the **Queen**, the Earl of **Leicester**, the Earl of **Oxford**, and the Lord **Admiral**, he goes on to state that not fewer than two hundred persons, thus retained and employed, strutted in their silks about the streets. . . The manner in which, about this time, the players were bribed away from Oxford is curious, and one of the items in the account expressly applies to the Earl of Leicester's servants.

So, acting companies did 'poach' from each other.

It is important to note that there were few London companies in which Shaksper could have gained experience within the late 1580's. He was not listed with the Queen's Men, and the Admiral's Men would not be a likely fit.

If one studies the number of Shake-speare plays and poems written by 1594, it becomes clear that we are looking at many works, developed over an extended period of time.

SHAKE-SPEARE PLAYS by 1594 – part 1

DATE	PLAY	COMMENT
1594	*Titus Andronicus*	Printed by John Danter 2/6/1594. Performed previously by Strange's Men, Sussex's Men and Pembroke's Men. Written? *Tittus and Vespacia* performed in 1592 by Strange's Men.
1592	*Henry VI, pt. 1*	Listed in Henslowe as *Harey the vj.* Performed by Strange's Men at the Rose. *Troublesome Raigne of King John* (1591) borrows from *Henry VI, pt. 1.* Not printed until 1623. Written ?
1594	*Henry VI, pt. 2*	Since *Henry VI, pt. 3* is quoted in Sept. 1592 (Greene's *Groats-worth of Wit*) pre-dates. Written prior 1592.
1592	*Henry VI, pt. 3*	Written prior 1592. Not printed until 1623 (first folio).
1589	*Hamlet*	Nashe alludes to *Hamlet* in preface to *Menaphon* by Greene. Henslowe's diary lists performance 6/11/94 by Admiral's / Chamberlain's Men. First printed 1603.
1594	*Taming of the Shrew*	Entered in Stationer's Register by P. Short. Performed Newington Butts 6/13. *A Morall of the Marryage of Mynde and Measure* — presented at Court 1/ 1579.
1594	*Comedy of Errors*	Performed at Gray's Inn 12/28/1594. Scholars date from internal evidence 1589-1593. Not printed until 1623 (first folio). In 1577, the play, *The Historie of Error,* was given at Court.
1594	*Merchant of Venice*	Henslowe, at the Rose on 8/25/1594, presented *The Veneyson Comedie*, an early version not extant. Entered in Stationers' Register 7/22/1598. First printed 1600. Early related plays? *The Jew* (1579) & *History of Portia and demorantes* (1580).

*=earlier versions which have been advocated as Oxford efforts.

35a. Shake-speare Plays by 1594 – part 1.

SHAKE-SPEARE PLAYS by 1594 – part 2

DATE	PLAY	COMMENT
1591	*King John*	Printed as the two part play *The Troublesome Raigne of John...* Lines mirror *Spanish Tragedy.* Condensed play not printed until 1623 *(First Folio).*
1593	*Love's Labour's*	Based on 1578 trip of Margaret of Valois to Nerac. Scholars based on similarites to *Venus and Adonis* and *Rape of Lucrece* date 1593 or earlier.First printed 1598. **A Maske of Amazones and a Maske of Knights* - Court performance 1/1579.
1591	*Two Gentlemen of Verona*	Dated per 11 years after London 1580 earthquake. **Felix and Philomena* presented at Court in 1585. First printed in 1623 *(First Folio).*
1594	*Romeo and Juliet*	First printed in 1597. Dated earlier by topical allusions.
1594	*Midsummer Night's Dream*	First printed in 1600.
1592	*Richard III*	First printed in 1597. Scholars believe written right after *Henry VI* plays as sequel.
1594	*King Leare*	Registered and produced in April by Henslowe.

Collaborations and prior Oxford efforts

DATE	PLAY	COMMENT
1590?	*Sir Thomas More*	See notes in text.
1586	*The Spanish Tragedy*	See notes in text.
1583-4	*Troilus and Cressida*	Edward de Vere presents **Agamemnon and Ulysses* and **The History of Agememnon and Ulysses* at Court.
1580	**(Twelfth Night)*	Edward de Vere presents "a pleasant conceit" at Court.
1578	**(Cymbeline)*	*An history of the cruelties of a stepmother* performed at Court. *The Rare Triumph of Love and Fortune,* performed at Court 1582.
1579	**(All's Well)*	*The historie of the second Helene* performed at Court.
1592	**(Henry V)*	*Harey of Cornwall* produced by Henslowe. *The Famous Victories of Henry V,* entered into the Stationers' Register in 1594.
1583	**(Much Ado)*	*A historie of Ariodante and Genovera* is performed at Court.
1579		**The historie of the Murderous Michael* performed at Court. An early *Arden of Faversham,* completed by Marlowe?

*=earlier versions which have been advocated as Oxford efforts.

35b. Shake-speare Plays by 1594 – part 2.

To accomplish work of this magnitude required an involved and stable London environment. Oxford's companies were the choice by default (for such activity), since other than the Queen's Men, Oxford's were the only companies available during the period that filled the bill.

Let's look again at what plays (later attributed to Shake-speare) have been printed / performed / concieved by 1594. If we peruse the preceding lists, we see they include fifteen Shake-speare plays.

To write these plays must have taken a bit of time. How far back into the 1580s did the process go?

Besides the fifteen plays listed, Shake-speare had also written *Venus and Adonis*, the *Rape of Lucrece* and participated in other collaborations, such as *Sir Thomas More,* and the early Oxford Court plays by 1594. Quite a catalog.

The previous two lists of plays point to twenty four plays in which Shake-speare had a collaborative hand by **1594**! The list could be extended. For example, Eva Clark's *Hidden Allusions in Shakepeare's Plays* points to evidence that the *Henry IV* plays were written and completed by 1592. Some Scholars have dated *Romeo and Juliet* to this period.

Perhaps everything in the prior lists were not Shake-speare collaborations. Perhaps there are other plays of Shake-speare (not listed) that were written by 1594. The point is that a large body of plays, plus the narrative poems were completed by 1594! **A number of these plays must have been written originally in the 1580s, or before**.

Shake-speare was hard at work in the 1580s. How does this fit in with early biography of Shaksper?

Rowe says, "[Shaksper] ...he is said to have made his first acquaintance in the playhouse. He was received into the company then in being, at first in a very mean rank." Dowdell says, "he run from his master to London, and there was received into the playhouse as a serviture." Davenant says (from a note in Edinburgh University library),

> Sir William Davenant, who has been called the natural son of our author used to tell the following whimsical story of him. Shakespear, when he first came from the country to the playhouse, was not admitted to act; but as it was then the custom for all kind of people of fashion to come on horseback to entertainments of all kinds, it was Shakespear's employment for a time with several other poor boys belonging to the company, to hold the horses and take care of them during the representation. By this dexterity and care he soon got to a great deal of business in this way, and was personally known to most of the quality that frequented the house; insomuch that, being obliged, before he was taken to more honourable employment within doors, to train up boys to assist him, it became long afterwards a usual way among them to recommend themselves by saying that they were Shakespear's boys.

Some comment on the above is needed (if this is true, rather than the poached-rural-actor hypothesis). London performances were during daylight hours and took up only a portion of the day. If Shaksper were earning money horse-holding, he was showing some of the skills, showmanship, and enterprise that was needed in the future 'artistic director' of the Chamberlain's Men. Many a budding author waits tables in our times to make ends meet. But what of Davenant? Pope says,

> Shakespeare, in his frequent journeys between London and his native place, Stratford-upon-Avon, used to lie at Davenant's, The Crown, in Oxford. He was very well acquainted with Mrs Davenant; and her son, afterwards Sir William, was supposed to be more nearly related to him than a godson only . . . That notion of Sir William Davenant being more than a poetical child only of Shakspere, was common in town; and Sir William seemed fond of having it taken for truth.

In 1780 Malone wrote,

> There is a stage tradition that his [Shaksper's] first office in the theatre was that of call-boy, or prompter's attendant; whose employment it is to give the performers notice to be ready to enter, as often as the business of the play requires their appearance on stage.

Moving from horse-holding entrepeneur, to call-boy, then to prompter would be useful experience for an enterprising, potential 'artistic director-writer.' The prompter was an important position. In addition to prompting, one kept the playbooks. Part of keeping playbooks was preparing manuscripts from the time acquired by the company through acceptance by the Master of the Revels.

The prompter hired playwrights, worked with the actors, revised dialogue, introduced humor, etc. The prompter was involved in the hire of costume and stage accessories. An enterprising prompter could own costumes, playbooks and be an important part of the company's management. Such a talented wit (who could write) would come to the attention of an interested patron-participant such as Edward de Vere. More about this when we get to the money trail!

A key component of a successful Elizabethan acting company was the prompter, since six different plays might be performed on six consecutive days. One play might be rehearsed in the morning and another performed in the afternoon. This is unlike modern practice at a major theater, where a period of rehearsal might be followed by previews and shakedown for a run of weeks or longer.

With little rehearsal, the prompter was the glue that kept the Chamberlain's Men productions on the boards. The prompter, play in hand, followed the words, action, and proper use of stage properties. Whispering the forgotten lines, getting the right actors and props on and off-stage were part of the daily responsibility of the prompter. This position at the heart of the acting company was an ideal place to learn and expand the practice of theatrical production.

KYD AND MARLOWE

Some scholars have described Kyd and Marlowe as precursors of Shake-speare. This doesn't square with the preceding datings. Of special consideration is the play, *The Spanish Tragedy* (attributed to Kyd), first printed in 1592 and written in the late 1580's.

The *Spanish Tragedy* has been noted for it's affinities in style, language and content to both *Titus Andronicus* and *Hamlet*. The *Spanish Tragedy* bears little in common with the one play certainly ascribed to Thomas Kyd, a 1595 translation of *Cornelie* by Garnier. *The Spanish Tragedy* went through nine printed editions from 1592-1633 anonymously (Kyd died in 1594).

In 1612, Heywood's *Apology for Actors* quoted three lines from *The Spanish Tragedy*, as by Kyd. Heywood did not say Kyd wrote the play, yet in the 1700s, on the basis of this quote, the play was ascribed to Kyd and he became a precursor of Shake-speare. Then Kyd became the author of the '*Ur-Hamlet*,' since it was uncomfortable to have *Hamlet* by Shake-speare being talked about in 1589.

During his lifetime, Kyd was berated by Nashe and others as a hack and for lack of knowledge as well as the inaccuracies in his work.

A point about *The Spanish Tragedy*. A key character is *Horatio,* as in *Hamlet.* This is a noteworthy coincidence. Kyd knew the Spanish and Italian languages. Spanish for Horatio is 'Horacio.' The Italian is 'Orazio.' Horatio, as previously discussed, was first used as a Christian given name in England by Horatio Vere, first cousin of Edward de Vere. It would be very interesting to find out if there were any other Horatios (people or characters) in Elizabethan times.

It is my belief that de Vere / Shake-speare collaborated with Kyd on *The Spanish Tragedy.* Also, Edward de Vere was the unknown patron of Thomas Kyd during the years prior to Kyd's death. When Kyd, under torture, denounced Christopher Marlowe, de Vere's patronage ended. Careful comparison of *The Spanish Tragedy* and *Titus Andronicus* reveals the thread of common authorship. There is also overlap between these two plays, and *King John* and the *Henry VI* plays. All of this is possible with the patron-collaborator, Edward de Vere.

Kyd, Marlowe, Nashe and Greene were in Oxford's literary circle in the 1580s. Kyd's testimony on Marlowe to the star chamber after both were arrested began:

> "My first acquaintance with this Marlowe, rose upon his bearing name to serve my Lord, although his Lordship never knew his service, but in writing for his players."

Kyd was admitting to his being part of Edward Oxford's household for over six years and that he and Marlowe wrote for Oxford's players in the 1580s. Marlowe's *Edward II* has affinities / overlap with the *Henry VI* plays. Charlton Ogburn's, *The Mysterious William Shakespeare* points to Marlowe's patronage by Oxford and how this resulted in the early printings of Marlowe's works.

A WEB OF ACQUAINTANCES

By 1594, we see that Shake-speare plays are being performed by Strange's Men, Sussex's Men, Pembroke's Men, The Admiral's Men, The Chamberlain's Men, Oxford's company, and at Court. Shake-speare certainly wasn't working as a playwright (or actor) for all of these companies. Published versions attested to the acting companies doing these plays. Access to the plays did not bring any outcry from the author. Perhaps the answer lies in the tangled web of patronage.

Edward de Vere (Lord Oxford) was befriended and championed by the Earl of Sussex (patron of Sussex's Men and Lord Chamberlain to 1583).

In 1595, de Vere's daughter Elizabeth married the sixth Earl of Derby. The Lords Derby were the patrons of Strange's Men. By 1590, Strange's Men had amalgamated with the Admiral's Men and toured in 1593, under the leadership of Edward Alleyn. By 1594, the amalgamation ended.

Alleyn then led the Admiral's Men. A second company, the Chamberlain's Men was formed (consisting of former Strange's Men) under the patronage of QE's first cousin, Henry, Lord Hundson.

Ill-fated Pembroke's Men was under the patronage of Henry Herbert (second Earl of Pembroke). Herbert was married to the literary luminary, Mary Sidney (sister of Philip Sydney). Lord Pembroke served with Lord Oxford at the trials of the Duke of Norfolk and Mary, Queen of Scots. Pembroke's son Philip later married Oxford's daughter Susan. Both sons Philip and William underwrote printing of the *First Folio* of 1623.

As we previously noted, the theater was a toy of the aristocracy. Edward de Vere, moving freely in his well connected circle, could very easily circulate Shake-speare plays to patron friends' companies.

So where did Will Shaksper get his training between 1585-1593? He was not with Strange's Men. In the traveling license of May 6, 1593, future Chamberlain's Men (Kemp, Pope, Heminges, Phillips, and Brian) are listed. Shaksper was not there, and certainly no Shaksper was in the Chamberlain's Men founders (1594). Nor was he with the Queen's Men.

Sussex's Men and Pembroke's Men were playing the provences before 1594. Neither they nor the Admiral's Men offered the stable training ground for creating the Shake-speare plays that were developed by 1594.

By process of elimination, only one place is left for Shaksper to gain needed experience; that is under the tutelage of and working with Edward de Vere's acting companies and at the Blackfriar's Theatre.

In the 1580s, de Vere had taken over Warwick's Men. He was staging performances at Court and the Blackfriar's Theatre. Oxford had in his employ secretaries Lyly and Munday, and was involved in writing / co-writing plays with Lyly, Munday, Kyd and his protege Will Shaksper. Oxford provided money, contacts, his library and his poetic vision.

Oxford caroused with the 'University Wits,' particularly Nashe, and provided accomodations at the bohemian 'Savoy.'

Yet the plays did get written, performed and were printed (printed anonymously through 1598). In 1598, *Love's Labour's Lost* was the first published play to bear the pen name, Shake-speare.

SOURCES FOR THE PLAYS – A LIBRARY

An extensive library of source material was needed to create the previously discussed plays, which were written by 1594. In an age with no public libraries, no computers, no typewriters and no ballpoint pens, where did you find the source material on which to base the plays?

PLAY	SOURCES

Titus Andronicus   Ovid's *Metamorphosis* in the original and Golding's translation. Seneca's *Thyestes* and *Troades.*

Henry VI, pt. 1   Holinshed's *Chronicles of England Scotland and Ireland* (1587). *Halle's The union of the two noble and illustre families of Lancastre and York* (1548). *Scot's Discoverie of Witchcraft* (1584).

Henry VI, pt. 2   Holinshed and Halle above. Foxe's *Book of Martyrs* (1563). Hardyng's *English Chronicle* (1378?-1465).Fabyan's *The New Chronicles of England and France* (1516).

Henry VI, pt. 3   Holinshed and Halle above.

Hamlet   Belleforest's *Histoires Tragiques*, v. 5. (in French) 1559-1580. Bright's *Treatise of Melancholy* (1586). Montaigne's *Essais* (1580). The Catholic burial service. *Ad Demonicum*, an Elizabethan textbook.

Taming of the Shrew   *The Arabian Nights. Here Begynneth the Merry Jest of a Shrewe and Curste Wyfe...* (c1550). Erasmus' *A Mery Dialogue...* (1557). Gascoigne's *Supposes* (1566).

Comedy of Errors   Plautus' *Menaechmi* and *Amphitruo.*

Merchant of Venice   Fiorentino's *Il Pecorino* (1558). *Gesta Romanorum. The Ballad of the Crultie of Geruntus.*

Troilus and Cressida   Chaucer's *Troilus and Crisyde.* Hall's tr. *Illiad* (1581). Caxton's *Recuyell of the Historyes of Troy* (1475). Henryson's *Testament of Cressid* (1532). Whetsone's *Rock of Regard* (1576).

Twelfth Night   Barnabe Rich's '*Of Apolonius and Silla*' (1581). The Italian play *Gli' Ingannati* 1537-85.

King Lear   Sidney's *Arcadia* (1590). Montaigne's *Essais.* (1580-1588). Holinshed's *Chronicles* (1587). Higgins' *A Mirror for Magistrates* (1574).

In addition, the 'Geneva' Bible (1560s), Blenhasset's *Mirror for Magistrates*, pt. 2 (1578), *Frederyke of Jennon* (1560), William Painter's *Palace of Pleasure* (1566-7), North's translation of *Plutarch's Lives*, Montemayor's *Diana Enamorada,* Boccaccio's *Decameron*, and Machievelli's *Il Principe,* and many other sources were used.

36. Shake-speare Play Sources to 1594.

This assumes you had the discernment to first select from the previous materials. Oxford's library / discernment is the answer that comes to mind.

Edward Oxford had been collecting books since he was a boy. There is documentation of the large amounts he spent on books in the records kept while Oxford was a Royal Ward in the care of William Cecil (Lord Burghley).

The previous list indicates some of the sources for the plays and poems written by 1594. The list is not comprehensive, but is an indication of the kind of books used by the collaborators in writing the plays. One should note that many of the books were older, out-of-print works. These were not the kind of books you could pop down to buy at the (non-existent) local Elizabethan bookshop.

Many Shake-speare plays were written by 1595. To write them required a good library. This writing was not the kind of output that could have been accomplished haphazardly on the road. Edward Oxford's companies were the most logical place for this activity to be happening in London.

SHAKSPER and the MONEY TRAIL

What about the money trail?

Will Shaksper's father, John, died in 1601. We do not have a copy of his *'Will,'* but he most probably left the bulk of his estate to his first born son, Will

Shaksper. John Shaksper began having financial difficulties in 1577 and had to mortgage and dispose of property. He never became a poor man, but had financial difficulties in his later years. Wife Anne brought Will a dowry of ten marks from her farmer father.

Shaksper had no fortune or trade when he left for London, yet by 1597 was able to purchase 'New Place,' the second largest house in Stratford-upon-Avon for £60. The somewhat delapidated house was then restored. With writers and actors receiving pittance wages, and Will having to maintain himself in London (even if he didn't support his Stratford family), how could he achieve financial success? Most likely, through the support of a generous patron, through business enterprise, or a combin-ation. Having financial acumen need not mean one has no artistic or poetic talent.

By **1592**, Shaksper was able to loan John Clayton £7 (almost a half year of an wages for an artisan). Amazing! A Public Records Office record shows that in March 1600, Shaksper sued John Clayton, yeoman of Wellington, Bedfordshire, in the Court of Queen's bench, for the repayment of a debt of seven pounds, acknowledged by Clayton in Cheapside (London's Eastcheap) on May 22, 1592. 'Cheap' meant market in medeival times.

Shaksper was doing well enough through pat-ronage or enterprise to loan out a substantial sum (sums?) in 1592. Also many Shake-speare plays and poems had been written. Shaksper was in London, he was part of the creative process and he had a patron. **If not, Shaksper was not Shake-speare!**

Much is made of the Third Earl of Southampton being Shake-speare's patron (on the basis of the *Venus and Adonis* and the *Rape of Lucrece* dedications). This is discussed and disputed later in subsequent chapters.

In any event, until 1590, when the Earl of South-ampton was seventeen, he had not been presented at Court or been a patron of the arts. If Shaksper was already in London and collaborating on the Shake-speare plays, he would have had to have already found a patron in de Vere. He would have been hard at work learning his craft.

Printing of *Venus and Adonis* and *Lucrece* would have been a costly business in 1593-4, without much potential for breaking even financially. This is not the kind of investment Shaksper, the realist would make. Not the kind of thing done to obtain a patron, either, since printing would have had to be paid for by a patron, or an independently wealthy free-spending-writer, like Edward de Vere.

Once Shaksper became a Chamberlain's Men sharer in the mid-1590s, his financial situation should have improved even more. Through care and frugality he could have parlayed his sharer portion into the stake for his further investments in the later 1590s and early 1600s.

What is clear is that between 1585 and 1594, a substantial part of the Shake-speare plays and poetry had come into being. Edward de Vere through his earlier work at Court, personal involvement, patronage of his prominent acting companies, library, contacts and support of writers, had a hand in this effort.

Will Shaksper of Stratford went to London and gained the experience necessary for him to become a member of the Chamberlain's Men. The silent pen of Edward de Vere and newly sharpened pen of Will Shaksper began transforming the Court plays of the 1570s and 1580s into what we know as Shake-speare.

One could ask why Edward de Vere, the Earl of Oxford, would collaborate with Shaksper? Edward de Vere was not the typical wealthy nobleman patron. He was a dedicated artist who associated with and supported writers and theater companies. De Vere flaunted convention. He occassionally acted on the stage, as in January 1579, before the Court.

De Vere had more writers dedicate literary works to him (many which de Vere paid for publishing) than possibly any other Elizabethan. De Vere surrounded himself with a coterie of talent. De Vere's circle of Nashe, Greene, Kyd, Marlowe, Lyly,

Munday, etc. was unconventional, rowdy, contentious, and known for their scandalous activities.

De Vere's group was opposed (in Court) by Leicester and his supporters such as Philip Sidney, Gabriel Harvey and Christopher Hatton. They berated Oxford and his circle, and conducted a war of words with them.

In the late 1580s, Oxford's cronies Nashe, Lyly and Greene, were paid by the Anglican bishops to castigate the Puritan pamphleteers. The Puritans, under the pen name Martin Marprelate, were distributing anti-Anglican pamphlets.

Nashe, Lyly and Greene went too far in 1590. In plays at Blackfriar's (using Oxford's Boys), they depicted Marprelate as an ape on stage. As a result, such a furor was caused that the Queen suppressed Oxford's Boys. Oxford had only one company left, Oxford's Men.

Edward Oxford spent time, much of his money and long-term personal effort on theater. Oxford encouraged talent and would have appreciated a witty, younger player-writer like Shaksper. Detractors of the Earl might characterize this relationship as stemming from the Earl's libertine, bisexual, nature. Perhaps there was or wasn't a physical relationship between Oxford and Shaksper. On this, there is no comment at this time.

What is known is that many of the Shake-speare plays and much of the poetry was written by 1594. This work required refining of earlier works, an extensive library of sources, collaborative hands aplenty, and the involvement of Edward de Vere.

Unless Shaksper collaborated with de Vere and contributed to this process, Shaksper would not have been able to gain the experience necessary to become the 'artistic director' / 'resident play-wright' of the Chamberlain's Men.

It is my belief that the collaboration between Shaksper and de Vere was forged in the later 1580s and continued to 1604 (when de Vere died). Shaksper's down to earth realism was the perfect foil for de Vere's elevated poetic nature. Collaborating transformed the work of both men. Together they could refine and develop their unique brand of theater; great theater which utilized all the talents of the 'dynamic duo.'

Point to ponder:

1. The years beginning in the late 1580s through 1604, led into and included the glory days of the Chamberlain's Men. Shaksper, working inside the Chamberlain's Men, together with Edward de Vere, his patron / collaborator, were the prime movers at the epicenter of this great artistic achievement – the golden age of Elizabethan theater.

7. SONNETEER SUPREME

Was Shaksper, de Vere, or both, the poet-sonneteer supreme? Before addressing this question, we should get a bit of perspective.

As previously indicated, the first time the *nom de plume* Shake-speare appears in print is in the dedication to the poem, *Venus and Adonis* (1593). To paraphrase the relevant dedication lines, "But if the first heire of my invention prove deformed, I shall be sorie it had so noble a god-father: ..." read, **if the first product of my pen name is deformed, I apologize, Southampton**.

The only other time the *Bard* used the name Shake-speare (in the works), was in the dedication to *Lucrece* (1594), which follows on the next page:

The terms in the dedication to *Lucrece* are so warm and familiar, that many scholars over the years have questioned the possibility of such a public display / offering being addressed (by a common-player) to a high-born aristocrat. Some wags have indicated that *Lucrece's* dedication would result in the immediate cessation of all social intercourse (at a minimum) between Southampton and low-born Shaksper.

It does seem hard to believe that Henry Wriothesley, the impetuous, class-conscious courtier, would accept such a dedication from a social inferior with equanimity.

TO THE RIGHT
HONOVRABLE, HENRY
VVriothesley, Earle of Southhampton,
and Baron of Titchfield.

HE loue I dedicate to your Lordship is without end:wherof this Pamphlet without beginning is but a superfluous Moity. The warrant I haue of your Honourable disposition, not the worth of my vntutord Lines makes it assured of acceptance. VVhat I haue done is yours, what I haue to doe is yours, being part in all I haue, deuoted yours. VVere my worth greater, my duety would shew greater, meane time, as it is,it is bound to your Lordship; To whom I wish long life still lengthned with all happinesse.

Your Lordships in all Duety.

VVilliam Shakespeare.

37. *Lucrece* – dedication (1594).

In any event, we propose that Edward de Vere was the official dedicator of these poems. De Vere may have written the poems himself or have had Shaksper involved in the project (as writer or co-writer). More about this later.

For his own reasons, de Vere wished to impress and expand his relationship with Henry Wriothesely, the nineteen-year-old, third Earl of Southampton.

De Vere and Southampton had similar histories. Both were high-born, lost their fathers early, became wards of Lord Burghley, were elegant gallants in their youth and became Court favorites.

In 1590, a match was proposed between de Vere's daughter, Elizabeth and Southampton.

De Vere named his newly born heir (Feb. 1592) Henry, as he did his earlier son (who died in infancy). Henry was a new name for the de Vere's.

There was also unsubstantiated gossip that Queen Elizabeth and de Vere were the parents of the Earl of Southampton (Henry Wriothesley). The rumor was this 'royal' baby was then substituted for the deceased newborn babe of Countess Southampton.

Shake-speare's reputation as a poet is based, to a great extent, on the 154 sonnets published in 1609.

Perhaps we should look at the overall poetic output of Shake-speare before addressing individual works. Figure 38 presents / describes known Shake-speare's poetic works.

SHAKE-SPEARE POETRY AND SONNETS

PRINT   TITLE / COMMENT
DATE

1593	*Venus and Adonis* - a narrative poem - approximately 1,200 lines.
1594	*The Rape of Lucrece* - a narrative poem.
1599	*The Passionate Pilgrim* - A collection attributed to Shake-speare - includes two later printed sonnets and other miscellaneous Shake-speare works, plus works of others.
1601	*The Phoenix and the Turtle* - printed as part of a collection.
1609	*The Lover's Complaint* - a poem appended to the *Sonnets*.
1609	*Shake-speares Sonnets* - 154 poems of fourteen lines.
1593+	Songs, poems and sonnets which are included in the Shake-speare plays.
1562	*Romeus and Juliet* by 'Ar. Br.' - a long narrative poem - a special case discussed in this chapter.

38. Shake-speare Poetry and Sonnets.

VENUS AND ADONIS

The poem *Venus and Adonis* was carefully edited by the Poet. The title page bears the Latin inscription (see figure 6), from Ovid's *Amores* which translates as follows:

> "Let the base crowd (common herd) admire what is low (common things) so long as golden-haired Apollo serves *me* cups filled with water from the Muse's spring (the waters of Casteley)."

Not exceedingly modest is it?

Venus and Adonis, the narrative poem of approximately 1,200 lines (in six-line stanzas), was tremendously popular in Elizabethan times. This highly erotic work was based on the Arthur Golding (1567) translation of Ovid's *Metamorphosis*. Arthur Golding (Edward de Vere's uncle and tutor) usually translated religious tracts. Racy translations were not Golding's usual fare.

It is possible that Golding translated Ovid at his teen-aged nephew, Edward's request, and that Edward participated in the translation. Certainly, this version of Ovid's *Metamorphosis* was a favorite Shake-speare source (as well as the original Latin).

Scholars have speculated that *Venus and Adonis* was written years earlier than 1593, and 'brushed up' for publication. De Vere may have written a version considerably earlier, that he, Shaksper, or both he and Shaksper 'improved.'

Richard Field (originally from Stratford-upon-Avon), who published *Venus and Adonis*, was apprenticed to the printer of three Arthur Golding works. Field bought John Harrison's firm (printer of a Geoffrey Gates book dedicated to / funded by Edward de Vere). Field had previously printed a fine edition of Ovid's *Metamorphosis*.

The 'grand gentlemanly' dedication of *Venus and Adonis* was not likely written to obtain a patron. Printing of the first edition of the poem would have been an expensive, risky investment; not the kind of thing attempted by a canny, money-lending, apprentice poet-theater person.

Most of what is said about *Venus and Adonis* is
applicable also to *Lucrece* (or *The Rape of Lucrece*
in later editions).

THE PASSIONATE PILGRIM
and
THE PHOENIX AND THE TURTLE

The Passionate Pilgrim, a volume of twenty poems,
was printed in 1599, by William Jaggard ("a
somewhat disreputable printer," according to *The
Reader's Encyclopedia of Shakespeare*). This comment is amusing since Jaggard was also a printer
of the *First Folio* of 1623.

The twenty poems, attributed to Shake-speare, in
The Passionate Pilgrim were:

1. Versions of sonnets 138 and 144 of Shake-speare.
2. Three lyrical extracts (poems) from *Love's Labour's
   Lost*.
3. Two of Richard Barnfield's poems from *Poems in
   divers humors*.
4. XIX is the first four stanzas of Marlowe's *Passionate
   Shepherd*.
5. XX is the first stanza of Raleigh's *Nymph's Reply to
   the Shepherd*.

We have listed five Shake-speare efforts, four by
other poets and eleven unknowns. Scholars have
been reluctant to ascribe the eleven unknowns to
Shake-speare because of their 'dubious quality.'
Were these early tryout works of the co-authors?

The Phoenix and the Turtle, by Shake-speare, appeared in a collection published in 1601 by Robert Chester. Jonson, Chapman and Marston were also contributers to the collection. Scholars have had problems with the meaning of Shake-speare's short poem, *The Phoenix and the Turtle* (67 lines). Maybe (or maybe not) the opening stanzas of the poem (which follow) will be more enlightening to contemporary readers.

The Phoenix and the Turtle

Let the bird of loudest lay,
On the sole Arabian tree,
Herald sad and trumpet be,
To whose sound chaste wings obey.

But thou shrieking harbinger,
Foul procurrer of the fiend,
Auger of the fever's end
To this troop come thou not near.

THE SONNETS

In 1609, *Shake-speare's Sonnets* were printed, and have been a scholars' field day (*cause celebre*) ever since. Figure 39 is from the first edition of 1609.

Note that the title page indicates, "Never before Imprinted." This is true, for the set had not been imprinted, yet versions (inferior?) of two sonnets had appeared in *The Passionate Pilgrim*.

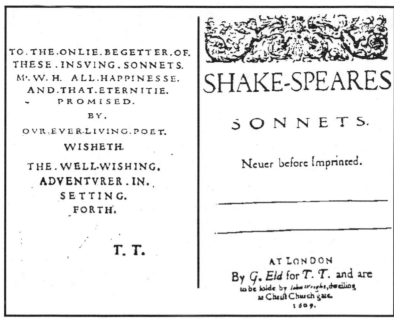

TO.THE.ONLIE.BEGETTER.OF.
THESE.INSVING.SONNETS.
M'·.W.H. ALL.HAPPINESSE.
AND.THAT.ETERNITIE.
‑ PROMISED.
BY.
OVR.EVER-LIVING.POET.
WISHETH.
THE.WELL-WISHING.
ADVENTVRER.IN.
SETTING.
FORTH.

T. T.

SHAKE-SPEARES

SONNETS.

Neuer before Imprinted.

AT LONDON
By *G. Eld* for *T. T.* and are
to be solde by *John Wright, dwelling*
at Christ Church gate.
1609.

39. Dedication and Title Page – 'Sonnets' of 1609.

The dedication has caused problems for many scholars who believe that "the only begetter," "Mr. W. H." was the 'fair youth' of the sonnets. Since the sonnets deal with other subjects than the 'fair youth,' this seems excessive. Master W. H., the procurer of the sonnets, was known to the publisher. The printing was not authorized. The following may add to the begetter mayhem. Shake-speare never used the word 'begetter' but did use 'begettest.' In looking up 'begetter' in the *Oxford English Dictionary,* it is also interesting that one 'A. Golding,' yes Arthur Golding (de Vere's uncle) is listed as a user of the word.

In any event (of more importance), the dedication includes the words, "OUR EVER-LIVING POET," which seems to indicate that Shake-speare is dead. I don't know of other instances of living Elizabethan poets being referred to as "EVER-LIVING." Does this refer to Edward de Vere, who died in 1604, as the sole-sonneteer? Shaksper was alive, so it doesn't make sense referring to him as, "OUR EVER-LIVING POET." Perhaps, it was assumed that Edward de Vere (died in 1604), who passed out the 'sugared sonnets,' was their sole author.

The following appears in Campbell and Quinn's *The Reader's Encyclopedia to Shakespeare*:

> The complete authenticity of the 1609 text has been repeatedly questioned. A number of the sonnets in the collection are of such an allegedly **inferior artistic quality** or ...dubious moral quality that they have frequently been assigned to other poets.

In reading the sonnets, I have trouble believing that a single poet would write so many poems (seventeen or more) urging a youth to procreate. That seems to be the message to the 'fair youth,' repeated *ad nauseum*, in the opening sonnets. Perhaps two collaborators were vying with each other to produce a 'winner;' or the person who collected the poems might have salted the mine (collected works or tributes by several poets).

Many poets were making tributes to the 'fair youth' of the sonnets (generally considered to be the 3rd

Earl of Southampton) in the 1590s. Perhaps Southampton collected these and they became part of the immortal *Shake-speare's Sonnets*.

Shake-speare poetry, unlike the encyclopedic plays, relies more on intuition and personal vision, rather than learning. The Shake-speare sonnets adopt an externally enforced older pattern (fourteen liners - abab cdcd efef gg). Are they really stylistically consistent? Even a consistent style does not guarantee a sole author. Style can be mimicked.

Edward de Vere could have set the 'style' for the Shake-speare poetry, then taught this 'style' to Shaksper. The mystery is whether the teacher or the talented student became the better poet.

For those who doubt that literary style can be learned, it must be restated that Shake-speare was imitated and mimicked repeatedly by Thomas Heywood and others during Elizabethan times. Today 'James Bond' and 'Nero Wolfe' mysteries (in the style of their deceased creators) are still published.

A LOVER'S COMPLAINT

A Lover's Complaint – a 329 line, narrative poem, was published in 1609 as an addendum to (at the end of) *Shake-speare's Sonnets*. The comments on the following quote from Israel Gollancz, in *The Works of William Shakespeare*, describes the poem:

In all probability the poem belongs to about the same period as The Rape of Lucrecc [1593-4?]... it's picturesqueness, versification, diction, repression, tenderness, and beauty, give it a thoroughly Spencerian character, and convey the impression that we have here an early excercise in **Spencerian style**; as such the poem links itself ultimately to the exquisite *Complaints* of Spencer's great master Geoffrey Chaucer.

So Shake-speare was working in Spencer's style in *A Lover's Complaint*. Perhaps we should experience the first stanza of this deathless verse.

A Lover's Complaint

From off a hill whose concave womb re-worded
A plainful story from a sistering vale,
My spirits to attend this double voice accorded,
And down I laid to list the sad-tuned tale;
Ere long espied a fickle maid full pale,
Tearing of papers, breaking rings atwain,
Stormin her world with sorrow's wind and rain.

What do we find in Shake-speare's poetry-sonnets?

1. *Venus and Adonis* and *Lucrece* – two longer, narrative, highly-stylized, erotic poems, based on mythology. These poems are always in print, but don't seem to be read in their entirety (except by specialists). If they did not bear the appellation 'Shake-speare,' would they remain in print?

2. *The Passionate Pilgrim* – a mishmash of five Shake-speare poems, four poems by others, and eleven orphan poems. Again, something that might not remain in print, without the author name 'Shake-speare' affixed.

3. *The Phoenix and the Turtle* – not exactly a world-shaker, except enigmatically.

4. *A Lover's Complaint* – a pseudo-Spencer-Chaucer romantic poem (of 329 lines) written probably by 1594.

5. *Shake-speare's Sonnets* and the appended *A Lover's Complaint* (romantic poem probably written by 1594).

Scholars have varied their dating of the sonnets but most believe the bulk of them were composed by 1594.

We indicated previously that a large number of Shake-speare plays (close to two dozen known works), were written / co-written by the year 1594. To this was added *Venus and Adonis* and *Lucrece*. It seems that most of the sonnets and *A Lover's Complaint* were also completed by 1594.

This seems an excessively large artistic burden to be carried solely on the shoulders of the enterprising youngster (not yet 30) from Stratford-upon-Avon, Will Shaksper. We suspect the project had been going on for some time, under the auspices of Edward de Vere, Earl of Oxford, and that Shaksper's unique talents were added to the mix. Determining which was the *Bard* is beyond the scope of *Who Were Shakespeare?*

Listed as a 'special' case in figure 38, is *Romeus and Juliet*. This narrative poem (3020 lines of pedestrian couplets) was printed in 1562, when Edward de Vere was twelve years old. *Romeus and Juliet* is the major direct source of Shake-speare's play, *Romeo and Juliet*. The title page and dedication of '*Romeus*' bear the abbreviated name

'Ar. Br.' (which possibly indicates a pseudonym). The poem is attributed to Arthur Brooke. Nothing seems to be known about Arthur Brooke, except that he 'died' after printing *Romeus and Juliet.*

Charlton Ogburn, *in The Mysterious William Shakespeare*, brings up the possibility that young Edward de Vere wrote *Romeus and Juliet* under the pen name, Arthur Brooke. The pseudonym may have used 'Arthur' for Arthur Golding and 'Brooke' to equal Lord Bulbeck or Brook (de Vere's title until he became Earl). This may be a little fanciful, but let's explore the background.

The year 1562 was a time of great stress and change for young Edward de Vere, who turned for support to his moralistic uncle, Arthur Golding. This is the year Edward's father, Lord John died. Edward became a royal ward (under William Cecil, later Lord Burghley). Edward was separated from his mother (who hastily remarried). He was removed from his home in Hedingham and rode to London, accompanied by 150 horsemen in blue Oxford livery. Edward had already matriculated at Cambridge, experienced world-class tutors, and been present at a state visit to Hedingham by Queen Elizabeth.

Edward was well acquainted with French. The source for *Romeus and Juliet* was Bandello's tale, translated in Belleforrest's *Histoires Tragiques* (1559). Figure 40 is a facsimile of a youthful letter (in French) by Edward de Vere.

The opening lines from *Romeus and Juliet* follow:

Amid the desert rockes, the mountain beare.
    Bringes forth unformed, unlyke her selfe her yong:
    Nought els but lumpes of fleshe withouten heare,
    In tract of time, her often lycking tong
Geves them such shape, as doth (ere long) delight
    The lookers on: Or, when one dogge doth shake
    With moosled mouth, the joyntes too weake to fight.
    Or when upright he standeth by his stake,
(A noble creast,) or wylde in savage wood,
    A doseyn dogges on holdeth at a baye,
    With gaping mouth, and stayned jaws with blood,
    Or els, when from the farthest heavens, they
The lode starres are, the wery pilots marke,
    In stormes to gyde to haven the tossed barke.

40. De Vere letter in French – 1563.

The dedication to *Romeus and Juliet* includes (among much moralization), the following:

> ... And to this ende (good Reader) is this tragical matter written, to describe unto thee a couple of unfortunate lovers, thralling themselves to unhonest desire, neglecting the authoritie and advise of parents and frendes, conferring their principall counsels with drunken gossyppes, and superstitious friers (the naturally fitte instruments of unchastitie)... Hereunto if you applye it, ye shall deliver my dooing from offence, and profit yourselves. Though I lately saw the same argument lately set forth on stage with more commendation, than I can looke for... which hath the more encouraged me to publishe it, such as it is.   Ar. Br.

One can almost see the youthful moralist of the dedication. Of interest is the reference to the stage. There were not abundant opportunities to see a London play in the early 1560s. Where could such a play be seen? At Court or a nobleman's house?

M. C. Bradbrook, in *The Rise of the Common Player*, gives few additional possibilities. For example Bradbrook lists a performance of *Gorboduc* at the Inner Temple in 1562, and discusses the forming of Dudley's Men in 1559. Perhaps there was more theater activity in London. The records of the Trinity Hall give evidence of an acting company back to the late 1550s.

Ward Elliot and Robert Valenza (at Clairemont College in California) have been experimenting with computer testing stylistic characteristics of Shake-speare and other Elizabethan poets. It might be of interest to test *Romeus and Juliet* against

Shake-speare's Sonnets. Are the family names Montague and Capulet (Capilet) in the Belleforest *Histoires Tragiques*? This is of interest because there don't seem to be any Italians named Capulet; and the Oxford English Dictionary defines 'capule' with horsey references. If the Montagues were a fiction of 'Brooke' in 1562, could he be referring to prominent Viscount Montagu (Anthony Browne, father of Countess Mary Southampton)?

In any event, there is the possibility (which could be further proven / disproven), that Edward de Vere wrote *Romeus and Juliet* under the pen name, Arthur Brooke. Edward may also have known Mary Browne (daughter of Viscount Montagu), four years his junior, from childhood. The poem *Romeus and Juliet* was published, apparently under author sponsorship in 1562.

SHAKE-SPEARE'S POETIC REPUTATION

Shake-speare's reputation as a superlative poet rests on:

1. The great sonnets included in *Shake-speare's Sonnets*.

2. Memorable songs, speeches, poems and poetic visions in the plays.

It seems that the proper question should not be, "Was Shake-speare's poetry a collaborative effort?", but should be, **"How much (individually or collectively) did Shaksper, de Vere and possibly others contribute?"**

8. CHAMBERLAIN AND GLOBE

Scholars refer to the Chamberlain's Men (CM) as 'Shake-speare's Company,' and the years 1594-1603, as the 'golden years' of Elizabethan theater. This is somewhat ironic since:

1. Will Shaksper was not (nor was Richard Burbage) on the original list of Chamberlain's Men shareholders / players.

2. There are no company records for the CM for the years 1594-1603. Perhaps such records were lost in the fire which destroyed the first Globe Theatre in 1613.

3. Many more non-Shake-speare plays were performed during these years (perhaps ten to one) than Shake-speare plays.

4. Only ten Shake-speare first editions of plays (mostly bad, unauthorized pirated versions) were printed between 1594-1603. This could partially reflect the CM's reluctance to authorize printing of their playbooks.

5. So much is made of the Globe Theatre (an outdoor summer theater finished in 1599), that it is hard to comprehend that the major portion of CM performances during this decade were <u>not</u> at the 'Globe.'

Shake-speare's reputation, based in good part on **posthumously published works** (the *First Folio* of 1623 in which seventeen plays were printed for the first time, and the *Shake-speare Sonnets* by the 'ever living poet' in 1609), has grown enormously.

Scholars have been heavily 'gilding' their picture of the 'golden decade,' a time of thin documentation. In this chapter, the CM staff, patronage and Shaksper's contribution are discussed. Figure 41 lists patrons, actors and theaters used by the CM.

ORIGINAL SHARERS PLUS

The original actor / sharers in the CM included John Heminges, Will Kempe, Augustine Phillips, George Bryan, Richard Cowley and Thomas Pope.

John Heminges (d. 1630) – was the actor and 'business manager' of the CM. Heminges acted with the Queen's Men and Strange's Men before the CM. He grew up in affluent circumstances. Heminges was included in a half dozen company acting lists and has been considered a tragedean. After 1611, it is believed he stopped acting and devoted himself to business affairs. Heminges was appointed executor /overseer of the wills of many

CHAMBERLAIN'S MEN – GLOBE THEATRE	
PATRONS and SHARERS	**THEATERS**
1594 Henry Carey, 1st Lord Hunsdon (original) Will Kempe, John Heminges, Augustine Phillips, George Bryan, Richard Cowley, Thomas Pope. (shortly after - Richard Burbage, Will Shaksper).	*Newington* *Butts*
1595	*The Theatre* (summer quarters - owned J. Burbage)
1596 Lord Cobham (at Hunston's death)	*Cross Keys Inn* (winter quarters)
1597 Geo. Carey, 2nd Lord Hunsdon	theaters closed (played provinces) *Curtain*
1599	*Globe 1 built* (outdoor performance) 1/2 owned by bros. Cuthbert & Richard Burbage and remaining half by 5 Chamberlain's Men: Shaksper, Heminges, Phillips, Pope, Kempe.
1603 King James Lawrence Fletcher, William Shakespeare (Shaksper), Richard Burbage, Augustine Phillips, John Heminges, Henry Condell, William Sly, Robert Armin, Richard Cowley.	
1608	*Blackfriars* (sub-leased for indoor shows)
1613	*Globe 1* (destroyed by fire)
1614	*Globe 2 built*
1619 King James (new patent) John Heminges, Richard Burbage, Henry Condell, John Lowin, Robert Benfield, Robert Goughe, William Ecclestone, Richard Robinson, John Shank.	

41. Chamberlain's Men – Globe Theatre.

of his fellow actors. Heminges is averred to have kept the CM out of trouble with the authorities. Heminges was co-editor of the *First Folio* of 1623.

Will Kempe (d. post 1603) – played the low comedy (bumpkin) roles for the CM until 1599 (when he left the CM). Kempe visited Denmark with Leicester's Men in 1585-6. Kempe acted in the style of the great comic, Richard Tarleton. Kempe was with Strange's Men prior to the CM. **Robert Armin** succeeded Will Kempe in the clown (fool) roles.

Augustine Phillips (d.1605) – Acted with Strange's Men prior to the CM, and appeared on Strange's acting lists. Phillips appeared on CM acting lists, and left (in his will) token amounts to his fellow actors, including Shake-speare.

George Bryan (fl. 1586-1613) – was a member of a company which visited Elsinore and Dresden in 1586-1587. Bryan was with Strange's Men prior to the CM. After 1596, it is believed that Bryan became a groom at Court.

Richard Cowley (d. 1619) – came to the CM from Strange's Men. Tall and gangly, Cowley has been proposed for roles such as Verges in '*Much Ado*,' Aguecheek in *Twelfth Night* and in *Julius Caesar*, Cassius. Until death, Cowley stayed with the CM.

Thomas Pope (d. before 1604) – toured the continent with George Bryan in 1586-7, and was with Strange's Men prior to the CM. Pope played high comedy roles and appeared on several CM acting lists. Witty Pope possibly created the Falstaff role.

Pope was prosperous at the time of his death and his will included shares in the Blackfriar's Theatre and Globe Theatre.

John Lowin (1576-1653) – replaced Thomas Pope in the CM. Lowin came from Worcester's Men. Lowin had a long career in the company, and took over some of John Heminges' business functions when Heminges died. Lowin was huge and corpulent. He performed Falstaff. Over twelve of his roles (bluff, outspoken parts) are known.

William Sly (d. 1608) – was in the CM from 1594-1605, and appears in all extant acting lists. Sly was with Strange's Men before the CM. Sly is reputed to have played youthful, romantic and soldierly characters in the CM productions.

It is interesting that at least three of the CM actors had visited Denmark and could have provided some first-hand background for the play, *Hamlet*. Also note that Leicester's Men was out of the country in part of 1585-6, and that the staff of the CM was fairly stable during the fabulous decade.

Only two actors (Kempe and Bryan) chose to leave the Company. For company stability, managers (cognizant of ongoing costs) often contracted with actors over a multi-year period in Elizabethan times. Leaving before your time often required payment of a stiff penalty.

The bulk of CM players came from Strange's Men in 1594. The Earl of Derby (Strange's Men patron), was (at this time) reputably the richest man in England. The Earl of Derby was a possible successor to Queen Elizabeth's throne. Derby and his heirs had to be politically careful to retain their heads. The Derbys' circumspection would have precluded support of a high profile company like the Chamberlain's Men and their potential political tinderbox (Shake-speare and other risky plays).

Ferdinand Stanley   (5th Earl of Derby) died in 1594, leaving Strange's Men without a patron. The company moved (under QE petition) to the patronage of Henry Lord Hunsdon (the Lord Chamberlain and Queen Elizabeth's first cousin). William Stanley (6th Earl of Derby), formed a provincial company, Derby's Men, shortly after the CM were formed.

BURBAGE AND SHAKSPER

Richard Burbage (1567-1619), the future CM star and leading tragedian did not come from Strange's Men. The Burbages were actors and businessmen. They owned The Theatre (CM's summer quarters). Richard operated such ventures as a livery stable, and also painted portraits. Richard was on good terms with his fellow actors even though he was their landlord. Shaksper made a token bequest to Burbage in his will. In 1591, Richard Burbage quarreled (over theater rent) with Edward Alleyn's amalgamated Admiral's and Strange's Men. The company left Burbage's 'Theatre' for Henslowe's 'Rose.' Burbage sought or formed a group to play the vacant 'Theatre.' In 1590, Paul's / Oxford's Boys and the Blackfriar's Theatre were suppressed. It is quite possible that Oxford's Men (including Burbage and Shaksper) became the 'new' troupe at The Theatre.

The collaborations later ascribed to Shake-speare, were underway by 1591. With Burbage, the lead actor-businessman, Oxford the patron-writer and Shaksper (the canny collaborator), much could be accomplished by 1594, when the CM was organized. Burbage, the congenial actor-livery stable proprietor, could well have befriended the writer-prompter-horse-holding-entrepreneur Shaksper. A reason that Shaksper and Burbage might not be on the original authorizing petition of the CM, is that they were already 'employed' by Edward de Vere, the one high-nobleman personally involved (to the destruction of his estate) in London theater.

CHAMBERLAIN'S MEN

The Chamberlain's Men had Burbage as leading man, high and low comics, soldiers, statesmen, young gallants, a Falstaff, etc. Even so, the CM staffing was pretty thin, except for the fact that players played two and three parts. Usually only two or three actors were on stage. Still, who played the women? Not Burbage or huge Armin. Not the tall, gangly Cowley. Perhaps the ladies were recruited from the suppressed Paul's / Oxford's Boys. Was Will Shaksper one of the ladies? No, Will, if anything, was an infrequent ghost or old king, etc. This seems in character, especially in view of Will's principal non-acting functions.

We propose that Will Shaksper was the astute prompter, play reviser, hirer of playwrights, and property manager of the CM. He might have made some additional money in dealing with the play-wrights and properties. Will, the witty, money conscious, occasional actor was essentially the 'artistic director' of the CM. Will revised or modified many a non-Shake-speare play for the CM. Will Shaksper also collaborated with his patron-mentor, Edward de Vere, on the plays which would bear the appellation Shake-speare.

Did Edward de Vere have more to do with the Chamberlain's Men than his involvement in the Shake-speare plays?

This is of importance since the facts of the Chamberlain's Men's success do not square with the details of their operation and organization.

Essentially, the story is that in 1594, the Admiral's Men (AM - formed years earlier) and the Chamber-lain's Men (formed in 1594), were for a decade, the leading London acting troupes. Both companies had indifferent patrons and were run by a manager (AM) or members (CM). The AM served as a vehicle for Philip Henslowe and his actor son-in-law, Edward Alleyn to become wealthy.

The Chamberlain's Men was run more demo-cratically by the artists and theatre owners for the benefit of the group at large. The Admiral's Men ran into trouble from time to time (individually and collectively) with the censors and authorities, while the CM led an unspotted existence (through internal efforts). All this in the rough and tumble, dog-eat-dog, suit-happy Elizabethan era. More had to be going on. Let's look again at the situation.

The patron for the Admiral's Men was Charles Howard (1st Earl of Nottingham and Lord High Admiral). Howard was patron of the AM until 1603, when King James I took the throne (and made his son Prince William, AM patron). Lord Howard commanded the English fleet against the Spanish Armada (1588) and was a cousin of Queen Elizabeth. In 1596, Howard and the Earl of Essex sacked Cadiz, Spain. Lord Howard, until he died in 1624, was involved in high level diplomatic and military matters for QE and King James.

Patronage of the AM was close to the throne. Henslowe and Alleyn used the AM to their great personal advantage, but had to operate within the restrictions of the times. To keep the audiences entertained (per Henslowe's records), the AM astonishingly put on 280 plays from 1592-1603 (including long non-producing intervals). Henslowe dealt with twenty-eight playwrights, many working in groups of two or three in writing / re-writing between 1598-1602. Of Henslowe's 280 plays, only thirty-seven were printed, which is not unusual, since approximately only 670 plays (out of over 5,000 produced) were printed from the 1500s to 1642.

Interestingly enough, the Cobham family was upset by the Shake-speare depiction of their Old-castle ancestor as Falstaff. The Cobhams paid the Admiral's Men to vindicate their name in the play *Sir John Old-castle*. The important Cobhams (former CM patrons) did not make waves for Shake-speare; most unusual.

Patrons of the CM were powerful and close to the Queen, yet seemingly indifferent to the acting company fortunes. Lord Hunsdon (CM patron) was a petitioner against CM use of the Blackfriar's Theatre. Most of the time CM patrons were off on missions abroad for QE, or suffering ill health.

In any event, the success of the CM was not due to their known patron(s). The Chamberlain's Men did keep out of trouble with the authorities, avoided the economically oppressive theater managers of the times, and had an extremely harmonious and prosperous run until Edward de Vere died in 1604.

Just a bit about these contentious times to put this in perspective – C. J. Sisson, in *Lost Plays of Shakepeare's Age*, discusses a long drawn out court case related to a marriage promise and woman's inheritance. The chapter on *The Old Joiner of Aldgate*, by Chapman, includes these complications which occured in the year 1603:

Milward... turned to the Star Chamber ... who prosecuted three considerable groups of defendants, accusing them repectively of conspiracy, perjury, and interference with the course of justice. ...and in the third we find three persons of the highest interest, a great dramatist, George Chapman, a theatrical speculator, Thomas Woodford, and the manager of a company of actors, Edward Peers, Master of the Children of Paul's. ...On the other hand, the relative credibility of John and Rose Oswald obviously became a burning question. And a platoon of Oswald's fellow-Stationers was doubled up to testify to his probity. Among them were some notable names, for the list of them includes Vincent Williamson, John Jaggard, the first John Harrison, John Hardie, Laurence Lysle, and Felix Norton. All depose that Oswald has been a good servant to the Stationers' Company...they defend him against accusation of drunkeness... Harrison qualifies: he hath seene... Oswalde many tymes merry with drincke, but never saw him very drunke to his knowledge.

Certainly the CM was run in a fairer, more democratic manner than other Elizabethan acting companies. During that contentious age, this is hard to believe (with knowledge of the printers, Shaksper's usury, Burbage's business ventures, etc.). It makes more sense if Queen Elizabeth exercised her influence through her former favorite courtier, theater-mad, Edward de Vere.

In 1586, tight-fisted Queen Elizabeth uncharacter-istically granted to financially strapped Edward de Vere an annual grant of £1,000. King James renewed the grant in 1603. The grant was unaffected by Edward marrying prosperous Bess Trentham (one of QE's ladies in waiting) in 1591. Edward de Vere did not perform known govern-

ment functions besides being on James' Privy
Council. Edward's major 'Crown' job was possibly
to produce propaganda plays. This evolved into
patron-in-residence of the CM. This would have
amused Queen Elizabeth and Edward de Vere
(among whose titles was Lord High Chamberlain).

The outside money, contacts and additional
involved patronage of de Vere would have been a
key ingredient to the success of the CM during the
magic decade. De Vere's clout and influence would
have helped with censors and those hostile to the
CM. The Shaksper / de Vere collaboration on plays
would have been furthered by de Vere's patronage.

Shaksper, working within the CM, tailored, adapt-
ed and made more stageworthy his collaborations
within the crucible of ongoing performance. De
Vere, reflecting and viewing the plays from the
audience, refined his contribution.

The Chamberlain's Men presented a wide range of
plays by a large number of playwrights in the
'golden decade.' They ran a purposeful group which
benefited the participants in an unusually harmonious (for the times) atmosphere. They were the
'top' company and became the King's Men in 1603,
with King James as their patron. This happened
when Richard Burbage and a talented company
teamed up with the master craftsmen of stage and
playmaking, the dynamic duo, Will Shaksper and
Edward de Vere.

9. THE DREAM TEAM

It is dogmatic testimony to man's love of a good myth (in lieu of facts) and his desire to be able to point to a sole creative genius (one man), that allows the ongoing story of one person being Shakespeare (the *Bard* who is world's greatest...).

Evidence gathered during the past four hundred years has pointed to collaboration in the Shake-speare plays and poems. Numerous writers have influenced (and numerous have been proposed as co-writers of) the Shake-speare canon.

There is much evidence documenting Shaksper and de Vere involvement in producing the Shake-speare works. Yes, they were the main creators, but who were their sometime artistic collaborators? Figure 43 lists some of the additonal writers whom scholars have depicted as Shake-speare co-writers.

We have seen that by 1594, versions of almost two dozen Shake-speare plays were in existence, as well as the bulk of the poetry. The internal evidence and older styles used in the plays reinforces dating them to the 1580s. The works were revised / co-written starting in the 1580s, with sources and older plays being collected as early as 1562 (the print date of the first edition of *Romeus and Juliet* - whether or not written by Edward de Vere).

Revision and rewriting continued until the printing of the *First Folio* in 1623. During this time (1562-1623) a multiplicity of hands contributed to the evolution, refinement and synthesis of Shake-speare's works. Contributing to this synthesis were dramatists, poets, editors, prompter/bookkeepers, printers, actors, copyists, the Revels Office, etc.

Figure 42 presents Shake-speare's Works – Authoritative Editions. We see that seventeen of the plays (almost half) were printed for the first time in the posthumous (to both Shaksper and de Vere) *First Folio* of 1623. There is no other authority for these seventeen plays or possibility for comparison, since we have no original manuscripts.

Let's discuss the seventeen plays which initially appeared in print in 1623, though these comments apply to all Shake-speare's plays. These seventeen plays appeared on stage at some time, in their earliest and later versions (revised / freshened). Throughout their theatrical run prior to printing, these plays received, at a minimum, the following:

   1. **Revels Office changes** – Each play licensed by the Revels Office (for a fee), might have text 'corrected,' if approved. Changes could be extensive. Charles Hamilton, in *Cardenio*, or *The Second Maiden's Tragedy* (for which the original manuscript exists) presents the play, including and noting the extensive changes made by George Buc, Master of the Revels.

SHAKE-SPEARE WORKS - EDITIONS OF AUTHORITY

WORK	EDITION - COMMMENT
All's Well That Ends Well	FF vile copy poorly edited
Antony and Cleopatra	FF (3,000 lines non-acting) well edited
As You LikeIt	FF good copy (promptbook source)
Comedy of Errors, The	FF (author's foul papers-draft copies)
Coriolanus	FF (contains printing errors)
Cymbeline	FF (promptbook or foul papers)
Hamlet	Q2- 1604 - corrected Q1+ foul papers
Henry IV, pt.1	FF - 1613 Quarto with oaths removed
Henry IV, pt.2	Q1 -1600 - good text from manuscript
Henry V	FF foul papers+ 1619 quarto (corrected)
Henry VI, pt 1	FF inconsistent 'composite authorship' (?)
Henry VI, pt. 2	FF corrected 1619 bad quarto
Henry VI, pt. 3	FF corrected 1619 bad quarto
Henry VIII	FF foul papers
Julius Caesar	FF long used acting script
King John	FF foul papers
King Lear	FF Q + Q2 + promptbook or Q1-1608 & Q2
Love's Labour's Lost	Q1 - 1598
Lucrece	Q1 -1594 (well edited)
Macbeth	FF promptbook (finished by collaborator)
Measure for Measure	FF bad copy - poorly transcribed source
Merchant of Venice, The	Q1 - 1600 - foul papers. FF from Q1
Merry Wives of Windsor, The	FF prompt book
Midsummer Night's Dream	Q1 - 1600 - foul papers/promptbook
Much Ado About Nothing	Q1 - 1600 - foul papers
Othello	FF acting version Q1 - 1622 promptbook
Pericles	Q1 - 1609. Not in FF-copyright problems
Phoenix and the Turtle, The	Q1 included edition 1601
Richard II	Q1 - 1597 foul papers or FF Q3,Q5 pr.bk.
Richard III	Q1 - 1597 and FF - requires both that differ
Romeo and Juliet	Q2 - 1599 - Q1 + foul papers
Shake-speare's Sonnets	Q1 - 1609 (many errors?)
Taming of the Shrew, The	FF promptbook
Tempest, The	FF cut to make room for maske-scribe trans.
Timon of Athens	FF foul papers, transcript, "strange jumble"
Titus Andronicus	Q1 - 1594 + manuscript
Troilus and Cressida	Q1 1609 and FF + additional hands
Two Noble Kinsmen (w. Fletcher)	F2 - 1634
Twelfth Night	FF promptbook
Two Gentlemen of Verona, The	FF promptbook (much abridged)
Venus and Adonus	Q1 - 1593 (well edited)
Winters Tale, The	FF - foul papers or promptbook

42. Shake-speare Works – Editions of Authority.
Note: __= printed first time in *First Folio* (FF),
Q=printed in Quarto format, and Foul papers
(author drafts) are scholars' guesswork.

In this instance such changes dramatically affected the play.

2. **Editorial changes** – Ben Jonson was editor of the Shake-speare *First Folio*. He introducd 'corrections' and changes to the texts.

3. **Printing changes** – Printers introduced a variety of changes into the *First Folio*. In typesetting, the spelling of words was altered to assist in making lines the proper length (justifying). Printers introducted transcription errors, and modified text on the basis of space availabilty. Of the 1,000 copies of the folio originally printed, over 225 remain in existence. These copies contain many differences and discrepancies, since corrections and changes were introduced during the print run.

4. **Transcription errors** in copying the source material. Sources for all the plays were hand-written copy. Many were from promptbooks or other material prepared by scribes. The accuracy of these copies varied. Scholars have indicated that the *First Folio* source of *All's Well That Ends Well* was a 'vile copy' which was poorly transcribed. This could also be said of *Measure for Measure* and other plays.

5. **Performance generated changes** – items introduced by the prompter-bookeeper and actors. The 'new' plays in the *First Folio* were produced many times over the years.

Actor staffing changes, theater changes, location (on the road or in London), performance time (limited time required abridgement, etc.), all had effects on the promptbook. Changes were made to court the audience, actor capability / availabilty, improve how a scene 'played,' etc. If a new actor couldn't sing the song interlude, it might be re-assigned to someone else in the cast. Scholars find evidence of all this in the acting version of *Julius Caesar* and other plays. What revelations would be provided if we could look at the promptbook and other sources of the *First Folio*. Alas, none exist.

So, the plays of Shake-speare underwent the modifications of the Revels Office (George Buc and others); editors of different editions such as Ben Jonson; printers and typesetters such as Jaggard and Blount; transcribers such as Ralph Crane, King's Men scribe; and those of the CM and KM actors, prompters and bookeepers. We have no original manuscripts to evaluate the extent of these changes. None of these changes are authorial.

After Shaksper and de Vere were gone, how many paid rewrites to freshen or make current for 'new' productions did these plays go through? How much was lost, changed or modified / 'improved?'

Before discussing co-writers Shakper and de Vere, a little background is provided with an excerpt from Charles Prouty's Introduction to *Mr. William Shakespeare's Comedies, Histories & Tragedies:*

...'Henslowe's Diary' ...a fascinating picture of the management of a theatrical company in **Shakespeare's London**... nine months from October 27, 1596 through July 28, 1597, the Admiral's Men presented 32 different plays, 15 of which were new and the remaining 17 were revivals... most popular play of this season was "Alexander and Lodowick", which was never printed and whose author is unknown... third... *The Spanish Tragedy* ...But even the blood, thunder, and rant of *The Spanish Tragedy* could draw an audience on only twelve occasions, and the constant demand for new plays is a dominant factor in the methods of dramatic composition...

How these men [Henslowe's playwrights] worked is equally instructive. In many instances they collaborated: Dekker for example worked with Drayton, Munday, and Wilson; with Chettle and Ben Jonson; with Chettle, Day, and Houghton; and on other occassions and in other combinations with Hathaway, Middleton, Smith and Webster. Dekker had a hand in some 44 plays during 1598-1602, and his total known output during his lifetime is in the neighborhood of 75; the actual total was probably much more... When we realize that but 17 of Dekker's plays were printed... only four by Henslowe... any more have perished. At least five plays for which Ben Jonson was paid have vanished... several thousand plays were performed of which we know nothing... We know Edmund Spencer wrote comedies but no trace of them remains...

...the disregard has been shown by the quotation from Sir Richard Baker who viewed actors and playwrights as "the meanest things." Attitude toward theatre is found in the "Diary" of Sir William Peter, a fashionable young man who frequented London in the last years of Queen Elizabeth's reign and the opening ones of King James's. Sir William meticulously records his gambling debts, his purchase of books, his wife's allowance, his expenditures for food, drink, and lodging, but there is not a single item listed for attendance at plays or the purchase of a printed play.

...it is reasonable to conclude that **Shakespeare's company** conducted their affairs in the same general fashion [as the Admiral's Men]. Both companies had to face the public demand for a large repetoire, some 30 to 35 different plays each season with one-third to one-half of this number being new plays, that is completely new plays or revisions of old ones... Recent studies have shown that a relatively small percentage of the public constituted the playgoing public... Never does Henslowe record more than two successive performances of a play... Shakespeare probably worked with other playwrights in his company, and that they, like those in the Admiral's, collaborated and at times revised old plays in order to satisfy the demands of the public... It seems to me incredibly at odds with the facts to suppose that a dramatic manuscript would remain unchanged from its first appearance as fair copy. Everything we know about theatrical conditions from Henslowe to the present day demonstrates that the texts of plays are constantly subject to change and alteration to suit the demands of the actors, whose last thought would be to preserve a pure original version. Thus it is apparent that the promptbook might differ markedly from the author's first draft or even the final copy he sold to the company.

The preceding parallels what happens to a present day film script, which makes sense. In any event, it was common practice in Elizabethan times to recycle plays and the names of plays (many alternate titles exist for the same play). The Chamberlain's / King's Men (to meet demand), put on hundreds of 'new' and recycled plays by the time the *First Folio* was printed in 1623. Most of these were non-Shakespeare plays, and an extraordinary amount of collaboration and play 'doctoring' occured in meeting the demand of the small and voracious theater-going public.

Will Shaksper, the prompter-bookeeper and 'Artistic Manager' of the CM, spent a good bit of his time dealing with plays produced (or rewritten) by hacks for the company. Most of these plays never made it to print or had more than a few performances. One can wonder how with such production demands, the Shake-speare plays came to tower over the 'hack' standards of the day?

If Will Shaksper had been working alone (bowing to cutthroat schedule and economic demands), the plays would be considerably more pedestrian. The factor of Edward de Vere's collaboration, for ego, artistic non-monetary bent, theater-madness or whatever, insured that the plays were considered more than ephemeral stage entertainments. This is why there is a non-stage (longer reading) version of *Anthony and Cleopatra*. It is hardly likely that this version would have been written by the busy CM playright. It wasn't written for publication since it barely made the *First Folio*.

Back to the sometime collaborators of Shaksper and de Vere. Figure 43 presents some of the Shake-speare collaborators proposed by scholars.

During the 1580s, Oxford's Boys and Men were performing in London. By process of elimination of other companies and the great amount of Shake-speare works to 1594, we have indicated that Will Shaksper was with Oxford's companies and began collaboration with Oxford. With whom were Shaksper and Oxford collaborating?

SHAKE-SPEARE COLLABORATORS?	
WRITER	**POSSIBLE CONTRIBUTOR TO -**
Fletcher, John	*Henry VIII, The Two Noble Kinsmen*
Kyd, Thomas	*Titus Andronicus, King John, Hamlet*
Munday, Anthony	*Sir Thomas More, A Midsummer Night's Dream*
Lodge, Thomas	*King John, Taming of the Shrew*
Marlowe, Christ.	*Richard II, Edward III, King John*
Thomas Dekker	*Sir Thomas More*
Nashe, Thomas	*Henry VI, pt. 1, Shake-speare's Sonnets*
Chapman, George	*Taming of the Shrew*
Lyly, John	*Comedy of Errors*
Chettle, Henry	*Sir Thomas More*
Wriothesley, Henry	*Shake-speare's Sonnets*
Greene, Robert	*Henry VI, pt. 1, King John, The Taming of theShrew*
Heywood, Thomas	*Sir Thomas More*
Earl of Derby	*Midsummer Night's Dream*
Barnabe Barnes	*Shake-speare's Sonnets*

43. Shake-speare Collaborators?

At Oxford's Boy's, John Lyly (Edward Oxford's secretary) was directing activities and writing Euphuistic comedies such as *Campaspe, Sapho and Phao, Gallathea* and *Endimion*. Scholars have suggested that the songs and other elements may be the work of Shake-speare. Lyly's plays influenced Shake-speare. Lyly may have collaborated on *The Comedy of Errors*. In any event, Lyly stopped his Oxford association and playwriting around 1590 when Oxford's Boys were suppressed for depicting Martin Marprelate on stage as an ape.

During the 1580s, Oxford's Men were performing in London and touring. They competed in London against the Queen's Men, Leicester's Men, and the Admiral's Men. Plays were supplied by sundry

playwrights including the 'University Wits.'
George Peele, Thomas Kyd and Christopher
Marlowe produced plays for Oxford's Men, as well
as being engaged in collaborations / rewrites on the
early Shake-speare histories and comedies.
Edward Oxford was their patron. Thomas Nashe
has been argued as collaborator on the *Henry VI*
plays and a version of the *Taming of the Shrew*.
Anthony Munday served as Oxford's secretary.
Munday wrote his first play for Oxford's company
in 1584. Munday influenced portions of *A Mid-
summer Night's Dream* and *As You Like It*. Robert
Greene has been proposed as co-author of the
Comedy of Errors and *Two Gentlemen of Verona*.

Of special interest is the play *Sir Thomas More*
(1590?). *Sir Thomas More* was submitted to
Edmund Tilney, Master of the Revels, who rejected
the play for passages containing controversial
content. These sections were re-written by several
writers. The original play was in the hand of
Anthony Munday. Additions were made by Henry
Chettle, Thomas Heywood, Thomas Dekker and
possibly 'Shake-speare.'

Thomas Merriam, an English scholar, did computer
stylistic tests of the play *Sir Thomas More* against
other Shake-speare plays and found the text to be
by the *Bard* (.25-.45 probability). Munday's plays
John a Cumber and *John a Kent,* when tested
against *Sir Thomas More,* resulted in probability of
the same author at .000000163. In *Sir Thomas
More*, we may have close to a Shake-speare fair

copy (copied by Munday), written by Shaksper and/or de Vere. Surely worth more study!

In any event, the Shaksper / de Vere collaboration began to change in the early 1590s.

Edward de Vere's life underwent considerable change in the late 1580s and early 1590s. Edward's first wife, Anne died and his children were cared for by their Burghley grandparents. Edward's affair with Anne Vavasor cooled and he bore scars, including being lamed in the vendetta with her family. From a first marriage marred by unhappiness and the spector of being cuckolded by Anne, Edward entered into a happy marriage with Bess Trentham, which produced his heir, Henry.

Oxford's Boys was suppressed. Lyly and Munday declined. Christopher Marlowe died, Thomas Kyd became an embarrassment, and the remaining 'University Wits' went their dissolute way. As a result, Edward de Vere began relying more and more on his diligent and witty star pupil-associate, Will Shaksper. Edward de Vere became more contemplative. He began downplaying Oxford's Men as a public company and folded much of the public company (including Shaksper and Burbage) into the Chamberlain's Men in 1594. Oxford's Men from this time on was primarily a private company that merged with Worcester's Men in 1602.

The collaboration between Shaksper and de Vere continued until Edward died in 1604. On de Vere's

side there was only the occassional co-writing of his
son-in-law, the Earl of Derby. Shaksper had his
hand in numerous plays as editor (*Locrine?*), re-
writer and co-writer (Fletcher on *Henry VIII*, etc.).

Shaksper and de Vere (together) created a body of
work greater than either could alone. They took
everything from ideas to complete works from their
fellow dramatists and reshaped them into
masterpieces. The de Vere library offered fodder for
their synthesis in everything from the 'Geneva'
Bible, to Ovid, to works on science and witchcraft.
De Vere's travel, entree into the Court and
aristocratic circles provided sources for caricature
such as the Burghley's, Christopher Hatton, Queen
Elizabeth, etc. Shaksper's knowledge of tradesmen,
farmers, usury and the commonplace, leavened and
expanded the universality of the joint output.
Shaksper, de Vere and their sometime collaborators
(writers of appropriated texts, co-writers, censors,
scribes, actors, editors, printers, etc.) over a period
greater than a half-century (1562-1623) synthesized and perfected to various degrees the plays,
poems and artist known collectively to posterity
under the trade name William Shake-speare.

A trade name? Yes, for no one seems to have
commissioned Shake-speare to write anything,
Henslowe never paid him/them for a play, and
Shake-speare somehow transcended the meanly
mercenary characteristics of the Elizabethan
theater milieu and the godfather of his name, Will
Shaksper.

10. The SPEAR-SHAKER

Edward de Vere, 17th Earl of Oxford, was a most unusual, multi-faceted, English highborn lord. He befriended writers and creative people of all types and social background. He spent his funds freely on the arts. The number and variety of dedications to him for works of substance (plays, music, scientific works, translations of classics, etc.) is perhaps the most impressive in the Elizabethan era.

De Vere risked his good name in personally involving himself in theatrical ventures (occassionally acting on stage, playing the fool for crowds during progresses, pouring funds into acting companies and writing / co-writing with his social inferiors). De Vere lived a full and exciting life (Queen's favorite, courtier, tournament knight, soldier, traveler, Romeo, playboy, pub crawler and swordfighter). He was neither angel nor devil, and was heavily used by the Cecil (Lord Burghley and kin) clan. A measure of the relationship between the Cecils and Edward de Vere may be gained from the inscriptions placed by Cecil on the tomb of Anne Cecil de Vere (Edward's first wife). The tomb contains statues of Anne de Vere and Mildred Cecil, her mother. The so-called sentiments of the three daughters (carved on the tomb) include:

> Lady Elizabeth Vere, daughter of the most noble Earl of Oxford and Anne his wife, daughter of Lord Burghley, born 2nd July 1575. She is 14 years old and grieves bitterly and not without cause for the loss of her grandmother and mother.... Lady Bridget... born 6th April 1584... hardly more than four years old... It is not true to say she was left an orphan seeing that her father is living and a most affectionate grandfather who acts as her painstaking guardian... Lady Susan... born 26th May 1587, who was too young to recognize her mother or her grandmother but is beginning to recognize her most loving grandfather, who has the care of all these children, so that they may not be deprived of a pious education or of a suitable upbringing.

This display on the tomb was penned by Burghley, the man who got his title so that his daughter Anne could marry Edward Oxford. Burghley milked Oxford and the royal wards for a substantial part of their fortunes; Burghley and his kin assiduously saved and edited their correspondence to show themselves off in a good light and hated Edward de Vere's theatrical endeavors. How much of de Vere's good name was tarnished at the Cecils' hands? How much of Edward's work was mislaid and/or lost through their efforts?

Was this all foretold in the stars? Edward's father, John and grandfather had kept an acting company of note at Castle Hedingham. In the summers, the company toured. Before 1509, Henry VII had commended the players of Lord Oxford, etc. In 1547, during the dirges for Henry VIII, Oxford's Men were causing a disturbance in Southwark.

Edward Vere
Lord high Ch
Married s:
W:m Cecil.
Eliz Daugh
of Roucc.
and died

42. Edward de Vere at twenty five years of age (1575).

So far we have discussed Edward de Vere's life to 1585. The following biographical outline describes Edward's life from then until his death in 1604.

1586   **8/26.** Edward is granted £1,000 annually by QE through Walsingham's Secret Service. This most unusual grant, with no strings, from the frugal Queen, is conjectured for production of patriotic plays (crown propaganda).

Angel Day's *The English Secretary* is printed with a dedication to Edward Oxford.

William Webbe says Edward Oxford is the "most excellent" of the Court poets.

Edward Oxford serves on tribunal judging Mary, Queen
  of Scots.

1587 **May.** Daughter Susan born.
Thomas Kyd member of household and Christopher
  Marlowe writes for his players?
Sep. Daughter Frances dies.
Sells two estates, acquires one.

1588 **June.** Wife Anne dies.
7/19. Commands his own ship against Spanish Armada?
Printing of Munday's *Palmerin d'Olivia* with a dedication
  to Edward Oxford.
11/24. Prominent Armada victory celebration. Edward
  Oxford carries canopy for Queen.
Dec. Sells Fisher's Folly and Vere House.

1589 Burghley sues for balance of marriage fee to Anne (dead).
Thomas Nashe in *Epistle* to Greene's *Menaphon* uses
  words "whole Hamlets of tragical speeches" referring
  to early version of *Hamlet* (Shaksper/Oxford?).
George Puttingham names Oxford as first among
  nobleman poets.
Marriage between daughter Elizabeth and Earl of
  Southampton unsuccessfully promoted by Burghley.

1590 Oxford's Boys acting company disbanded.
Fall: Writer Churchyard lodges at Edward Oxford's
  expense.

1591 Edward marries Elizabeth Trentham, a wealthy Maid of
  Honor to the Queen.

1592 Lyly's playwriting career over.
Aug. Present at banquet with writers Greene and Nashe.

1593 Nashe's *News* printed with dedication to Edward Oxford.
2/24. Son and heir Henry born.

1594 **Apr.** *King Leare* registered and performed two days later.
  An early Shaksper/Edward Oxford version?
A version of *Hamlet* is produced by Henslowe. An early
  Shaksper/Oxford version?
Sep. *Willobie* verse on Shake-speare.

1595 **Jan.** Daughter Elizabeth marries 6th Earl of Derby.
Sep. Receives thank you letter from French king.

1596 Settles into King's Place, Hackney, with wife and son.

1597 Lord and Lady Pembroke (Mary Sydney) seek his
  daughter Bridget's hand for their son.

45. Brooke Place (former King's Place, Hackney) 1761.

1598   9/7. *Pallas Tamia* by Francis Meres registered. Names
Edward Oxford best for comedy, and has an extensive
listing for Shake-speare.

1599   Printing of John Farmer's *Set of English Madrigals*
dedicated to Edward Oxford.
Queen permits Oxford a third London acting company.

1601   Serves on treason tribunal of the Earl of Essex.

1602   IIis Company and Worcester's combine in third London
acting company performing at the Boar's Head in
Cheapside, haunt of *Falstaff* and *Prince Hal*. Queen
Elizabeth dies, King James crowned.

1603   His company taken over by Queen Anne, wife of James I.
July. King James renews his munificent annuity of
£1,000 (literary purposes?).

1604   6/24. Dies of plague. Buried Hackney church 7/6.

Edward wrote poetry into his twenties (anonymously, pseudonomysly). The first verse of the
early poem *Loss of Good Name* follows:

LOSS OF GOOD NAME by Edward Oxford

> Fram'd in the front of forlorn hope, past all recovery,
> I stayless stand, to abide the shock of shame and imfamy.
> My life, through ling'ring long, is lodg'd in lair of loathsome
>   ways;
> My death delay'd to keep from life the harm of hapless days;
> My sprites, my heart, my wit and force, in deep distress are
>   drown'd;
> The only loss of my good name is of these griefs the ground.

Anne Vavasor, Edward's paramoor and mother of his illegitimate son Edward Vere, wrote poems to the Earl. Anne may have been the dark lady of the sonnets. Eight years after birthing Edward Vere, she had another natural son who bore the name Thomas Vavasor (later Thomas Freeman). After numerous scandalous affairs, Anne married a sea captain (Thomas Finch) then left him for the aged Sir Henry Lee (retired Queens Champion) and stayed with Henry for twenty years (until Henry died). Anne who lived into her nineties was referred to as 'that drab' by Lord Burghley. Certainly Anne Vavasor was more colorful and devious than this poem (two of seven stanzas) by her to Edward de Vere would indicate:

Anne Vavasor poem to Edward de Vere

> Tho' I seem strange, sweet friend, be thou not so.
> Do not accoy thyself with sullen will;
> Mine harte hath vowed, although my tongue says noe,
> To be thine own in friendly liking still.
>
> Thou seest me live amongst the lynxes' eyes
> That pry into the privy thoughts of mynde;
> Thou knowst right well what sorrows may arise
> If once they chance my settled looks to find.

44. Anne Vavasor.

Stage-struck Edward de Vere lived a life that was much like a play in which he starred. Born into wealth and privilege, he enjoyed falconry and hunting with his father. He received a first class education. At age twelve, his father died. He became a ward of Lord Burghley and began his London residence. He began buying books in his teens. His 'Geneva' Bible contains a number of underlined passages with marginal notes. A high correlation exists between these passages and their use in Shake-speare plays. Did de Vere, Shaksper, or both make the markings in the 'Geneva' Bible?

De Vere wrote plays (for Court performance, etc.) and poetry in the 1570s. Some of the poems and over fifty letters of de Vere are still in existence. In the 1580s, he supported acting companies and hired writers such as Lyly, Munday, Peele, Nashe, Kyd, Marlowe and Greene. De Vere helped publish these writers' plays and collaborated with them on revising his early plays for Oxford's Men / Boys.

De Vere and his group were well on the way to synthesizing the Shake-speare style. They revamped the early versions of many of the plays that de Vere wrote in the 1570s, saw, or for which he collected source materials and books. Will Shaksper joined the venture at the critical time he would benefit from learning and working with his patron-collaborater, de Vere. Will provided much, including the leavening necessary for universal appeal.

De Vere worked as a co-writer until his death in 1604. The last years of his life were spent writing, working with theater staff and living quietly in his Hackney home, King's Place. This residence stood until the 1950s, when it was demolished.

De Vere, the courtier, Queen's favorite, ladies man, dissolute theater person (who frequented the company of the 'University Wits'), traveler-adventurer, generous-spendthrift patron, was now mellowing. Adventures with pirates, shipwrecks, dalliance in foreign Courts, gossip about highly placed individuals and petty feuds, such as the tennis altercation with Philip Sidney, were now past. This life experience upon reflection became grist for de Vere's playwriting collaborations.

11. SCHOOL OF SHAKE-SPEARE

During the renaissance (15th and 16th centuries), to become an artist, one was apprenticed to a master. The painter Perugino was the teacher of Raphael. Raphael travelled to Perugia, did his stint as an apprentice, created a 'masterpiece' and in time developed a greater luster through his creations than did his teacher. Often a master developed a unique style of painting that his students emulated. When a discernable style was practised by a group (often indistiguishable as individuals) it became known as 'school of...' Many a well known Rembrandt, housed in a prestigious museum, has become, after careful scientific scrutiny during the last century, a 'school of Rembrandt' painting.

The **School of William Shake-speare** might be an appropriate way of describing the authors of the Shake-speare plays and poems. For a period of over half a century (1562-1623), the source materials were gathered, works were written and re-written by the authors. In the censorship-performance-publishing crucible, the works became homogenized and altered / synthesized into the *First Folio* of 1623 and an armful of Quartos (which were often contradictory, printed editions).

No original authorial source materials are available. What should and should not be included in the canon continues to be disputed. How much of what we have is by the original author(s)? Roughly fifty percent, or twenty-five percent, or seventy-five percent? No one really knows. How much of what we have of Shake-speare is trash and how much treasure? This should be addressed more fully. How much of the school of Shake-speare was there that has been lost?

It is beyond the scope of *Who Were Shakespeare?* to answer these questions. In this work we have tried to show that:

Will Shaksper, the extremely talented, modestly educated, witty young man from Stratford-upon-Avon, left for London in the mid-1580s, leaving his wife and children behind. Without a trade or independent means, he gravitated to money-making activities in the theater district, and became a member of a theater company (Oxford's Boys – Oxford's Men).

Prior to this time (1585) Edward de Vere, 17th Earl of Oxford had been receiving a superb education, writing plays and poetry, supporting and participating in acting companies, occasionally acting on stage, clowning in public, hiring / associating with writers, buying a library of books, traveling and gaining a wide range of life experience.

In the mid-1580s, Edward de Vere, the master, became the patron-teacher of his brash young collaborator, Will Shaksper. Will worked hard at learning everything he could about theater from his teacher, de Vere, and colleagues in Oxford's companies. Through prompting, play revision, wheeling-and-dealing in properties and working with playwrights, Will's writing skill increased. Old 'so-so' de Vere Court plays, and many an anonymous nondescript play passed through the hands of Will and his co-writer, Edward de Vere. Such was necessary to satisfy the public attending performances of Oxford's Men. De Vere published *Venus and Adonis* and *Lucrece* with the dedication bearing the invented name William Shake-speare (whether written by de Vere, Shaksper, or both).

Things changed in the 1590s. De Vere began de-emphasizing the public performance aspects of Oxford's Men, his coterie of writers dispersed, and he now had a happy home life. London public theater developed. The relationship of collaboration between Shaksper and de Vere strengthened and became a collaboration of artistic equals who recognized each other's unique talents and contributions. In 1594, with the formation of the Chamberlain's Men, de Vere melded Shaksper, Burbage and the promptbooks, etc. of Oxford's Men into the new company.

During the next decade, Shaksper from within the Chamberlain's Men, and de Vere from without, refined and wrote / rewrote the plays. Shaksper became the prompter-bookeeper and 'Artistic Director' who very occasionally acted. He was the middle man in buying plays from playwrights and also rewrote plays. Will engaged in earning money and artistic adventures and amassed the lucre to eventually return as a gentleman to his beloved Stratford. De Vere, beside writing / co-writing, retained his status as mentor, financial supporter, library source, and 'in' to the aristocracy.

After 1604 (when de Vere died), Shaksper continued in an ever-decreasing level at the King's Men. Newer playwrights like Beaumont and Fletcher began to prevail. However, there continued to be collaboration with Will, and the Shake-speare plays underwent revision.

What we have presented as the school of William Shake-speare may be divided into four periods:

Preparation or gathering (1562-1585) – From the gathering of *Romeus and Juliet* in 1562 and other poetry, printed material, plays and early writings of Edward de Vere.

Melding of minds (1586-1593) – The addition of Shaksper to the mix, training of Shaksper and evolution of the Shake-speare style.

Creative flowering (1594-1603) – The mix of collaborative genius and high-powered acting organization bears fruit.

Decline and dogmatizing (1604-1623) – Modification of existing works and setting the mold (though what remains is uneven, error laden and inconsistent) is done largely through the *First Folio* (1623), *Shake-speare's Sonnets* (1609) and an armful of Quartos.

After all this, there will still be those who insist that Will Shaksper was the sole author, William Shake-speare. To these people we say, **Will was born too late** (1564) to be the sole author. By the time that Will saw the Stratford Grammar School (the 1570s), the School of Shake-speare had already been established. By the time Will arrived in London (the 1580s), the style, sources and versions of the early plays by de Vere and Oxford's Mens' writers existed. Will did not have the theater knowledge and training necessary to lead the 'school' when he arrived in London. Will would have had to start as an apprentice to the master (de Vere). In addition, Will lacked the broad education, library, contacts, Court insider experience, and travel / life experience necessary for the sole writing of the plays (a virtual 'Encyclopedia Elizabetheana'). When Will Shaksper arrived in London, he used his ingenuity, determination and cunning to set up a theatrical horse-holding enterprise. He entered the service (theater activities) of his patron, Edward de Vere, and over time became became a valued co-writer of the Shake-speare plays. By 1592, Will's activities (business, patronage funded, and prompting-writing) allowed him to engage in money lending (per the Clayton suit). After the Chamberlain's Men was formed, Will was talented and exper-ienced enough to join the company as prompter-bookkeeper and 'Artistic Director.' Will's col-laboration with de Vere continued with spectacular results.

There are those who will still maintain that Edward de Vere, 17th Earl of Oxford, was the sole writer who wrote under the pen name, William Shake-speare. They would also conclude that Will Shaksper was merely a straw-man / front for the author. This does not square with what is known. Will Shaksper became a sharer and part owner in the Chamberlain's Men, King's Men, Globe Theatre and Blackfriar's Theatre. It would have been extremely foolhardy to place a straw-man within the leading acting company of the era. Exposure of the straw-man's ineptness would have been inevitable. It would have become obvious to CM members that Shaksper was not 'the' writer. Certainly, the company sharers would have ob-jected to a straw-man owning a share of their playhouses. The Shake-speare plays reflect the hand of a person involved in day-to-day theater activity (Shaksper the prompter-bookeeper and 'Artistic Director' of the CM). The plays are leavened with an earthy bawdiness and vivid depictions of all strata (including lower and middle levels) of Elizabethan society. Edward de Vere had catholic talents / interests, but did not have the non-aristocratic experience necessary to solely weave the colorful tapestry of the Shake-speare plays.

The collaboration of Shaksper and de Vere was a fortuitous fluke of history. Two very different, extremely talented men were able to work together to produce something better than they could individually. Their efforts became the foundation for the School of Shake-speare.

What has happened over time to the Shake-speare canon is similar to what has happened to 'classical music.' Elizabethan public theater and Mozart public concerts were popular fare in their time. From the 1500s to the 1700s, musicians, like Elizabethan actors were either servants of the nobility or the church (as was Bach). Plays and music performed were usually not well rehearsed. Musicians and actors would often ad-lib their parts. Works were written for performance, and altered for the actors / musicians available, and their varying abilities. Mozart improvised his cadenzas. Bach participated in improvisation competitions. The quality of performer training and quality of theater / equipment was not up to modern standards.

It would not be an exaggeration to say that the works of Elizabethan playwrights (such as Shake-speare) and the non-keyboard music of 'classical composers' (sixteenth to eighteenth century) are currently routinely performed by professional organizations at a higher quality than was ever attained during their creators' lifetimes.

Scholars over the centuries have attempted to find the definitive Shake-speare playscript and Mozart performance style. From these attempts we gain a certain stylized, rigid product of high quality. Fortunately, there are always those performers who experiment and attempt to bring back the fluid flavor of the original work. Also, our old masters are used and misused by popular media. Who has not seen a television commercial accompanied by fragments of Rossini's *William Tell Overture*, heard a blaring rock version of *Beethoven's Fifth Symphony*, or viewed a tee-shirt sporting the Martin Droeshout fantasy version of William Shake-speare?

Will Shaksper (Shax-pair) and Edward de Vere became William Shake-speare (Shiek-spair). Their work, with help from additional hands, became the bedrock of the School of Shake-speare. De Vere and Shaksper were poets (perhaps rival poets), and one or both of them is/are revered as the *Bard*. Each man contributed his special talents and genius to co-writing the Shake-speare plays. England, the country which produced Gilbert and Sullivan, ought to be able to take in stride Shaksper and de Vere, collaboratively known as William Shake-speare.

APPENDIX A

TEN MYTHS REVISITED

Myths which have contributed to obscuring the true authorship of the Shake-speare works follow:

1. The sole creator myth – that the works bearing the author name 'William Shake-speare' are the work of one person. *Who Were Shake-speare?* presents extensive evidence debunking this myth.

2. The name myth – that the names Shaksper and Shake-speare were pronounced the same way and thought to be the same name / person in Elizabethan times. We have shown that Shaksper was pronounced Shax-pair, while Shake-speare was pronounced (the 'ie' as in lie) Shiek-spair. The reason for the hyphen was to insure breaking the syllables between the 'e' in Shake and 's' in speare, thereby emphsizing the two words.

3. Shaksper the man was known as 'the' writer. In Elizabethan times it was not known that Will Shaksper of Stratford-upon-Avon, and William Shake-speare were the same person. This is a later invention. We have shown that such did not occur to the chronicler, Camden, who knew Will Shaksper, had a high regard for the writing of

William Shake-speare, and did not connect the two as the same person.

4. Will Shaksper was an actor. There is little support for the myth that Will Shaksper was an actor, other than the mention that he may have played the part of a ghost or old king. This is consistent with his role as prompter-keeper of playbooks / 'artistic director.' The one greatly over-used source for this assumption is Greene's *Groats-worth of Witte*, discussed in item seven.

5. Will Shaksper was a known playwright in 1592. The *nom de plume* William Shake-speare was not used until 1593, in the dedication to *Venus and Adonis*, which indicated this was the first use of the invented name (pen name) Shake-speare. The first use of the name on a play was in 1598, the year of Meres' *Palladis Tamia*. In 1592, the anonymous plays later ascribed to Shake-speare were not ascribed publicly to Shaksper or anyone else. See also item seven dealing with Greene's *Groats-worth of Witte*.

6. Will Shaksper was a sharer in the Chamberlain's Men in 1594. The derivation of this myth is from the accounts of Queen Elizabeth's Treasurer of the Chamber, for 1594-1595. The Treasurer made payments to players, etc., for Court performances arranged by the Revels Office. The entry reads, "To Will Kempe Willm Shake-speare & Richard Burbage seruantes to the Lord Chambleyne vpon the councelles warrt dated at

Whitehall   XVto Martii 1594 for twoe seuerall
comedies or Enterludes shewed by them before her
Matte in xpmas time laste...upon St. Stephens day
and Innocents day." This record was not prepared
by Sir Thomas Heneage (one of QE's favorite
courtiers), since he died in 1595. In 1594, Heneage
had married the widow of the 2nd Earl of
Southampton (Mary Browne). Charlotte Stopes has
documented that widow Heneage had received a
nasty note requesting an accounting from Queen
Elizabeth.

Thereupon widow Heneage wrote/rewrote the late
1594-1595 entries for the Treasurer of the
Chamber. These included the £20 to the Chamberlain's Men performance on Innocents Day
(December 28th). Incidentally, the Admiral's Men
performed for the Queen on Innocent's Day, while
the Chamberlain's Men performed in Greenwich.
Widow Heneage knew of Shake-speare.

Widow Heneage rewrote her dead husband's records to reduce personal liability and mollify the
Queen. Shaksper may or may not have been with
the CM, or a sharer at this time (the time widow
Heneage indicated). Certainly this record is suspect
and without corroboration should not be taken as
proof.

7. Accurate creation dates for the plays.
Dating of the plays has been influenced by the
myth of Shaksper being the sole creator. Scholars
starting with this assumption have had to reason

that Shaksper was born in 1564, arrived in London 1585 or later, had to get years of training, therefore couldn't have written plays much before 1590. While Shaksper died in 1616, it seems that Shaksper spent most of his time in Stratford-upon-Avon after 1604. Since this leaves only a fifteen year window (1589-1604) for all the writing, Shaksper's retirement has been postponed.

The *First Folio* of 1623, included seventeen plays printed for the first time. Play printing dates and spotty performance records available are not a good indicator of when plays were written. This is why internal / stylistic evidence of the earlier dates for play creation are ignored.

There is evidence for *Hamlet* being performed in 1589 (as mentioned in Nashe's preface to *Menaphon*), and in 1594 (in a performance noted in Henslowe diaries). Such are written off as the non-Shake-speare *'Ur-Hamlet'* by Kyd. This doesn't make much sense when Shake-speare's *Hamlet* was printed in 1603. The play must have been performed and written years before 1603. If *Hamlet* were first presented in 1589 it would have had fifteen years to be perfected / re-written and improved. This would not be unusual.

8. Southampton was Shaksper's patron. This myth is based on the dedications to Southampton in *Venus and Adonis* and *Lucrece*. There is no other corroboration for this myth. The height of the myth is (the invention) that Southampton gave Shaksper

£1,000. Shaksper never received such a lump sum. If he had, he would have packed his bag and retired immediately to Stratford-upon-Avon. The wording of the *Lucrece* dedication from an older commoner to a younger aristocrat would not have been tolerated. Shaksper may have had a hand in the poems, but he did not pay for the printing, nor was he the official person dedicating the poems. Shaksper had business interests, a patron, or both in 1592 (before the dedications), when he loaned money to John Clayton.

9. The *First Folio* of 1623 is a completely reliable source. The *First Folio* is the only available source for much of Shake-speare's work. The work was edited by Ben Jonson, a rival playwright. The folio was inaccurate in attesting to contain all of Shake-speare's plays. *Pericles* (because of copyright problems) was not included. What was included is what was available. The sources were not always the best. It is possible that **not one original authorial** manuscript was used in preparing the manuscript. How much was lost in the burning of the first Globe Theatre (1613)? In 1621, the Fortune Theatre (home of the Admiral's Men) burned. The fire and effect on the company is described in the following (John Chamberlain) letter excerpt.

> On Sunday night here was a great fire at the Fortune in Golden-Lane, the fayrest play-house in this towne. It was quite burnt downe in two howres, & all their apparell & play-bookes lost, whereby those poor companions were quite undone.

Jonson's comments on Shake-speare are suspect, as
is Jonson's listing of Shake-speare at the head of
the list of actors performing the plays. What
editorial changes Jonson made to the plays is
unknown. In any event, when using the *First Folio*
as a source, one should be wary of the promotional
and self-serving nature of the non-play material.

10.   Chettle's Chuckle. Much has been er-
roneously adduced from Robert Greene's *Groats-
worth of Witte*, (1592). First of all, it has been
questioned whether this pamphlet was written on
his deathbed by Robert Greene. Henry Chettle may
have penned the pamphlet, or the pamphlet may
have been written earlier than 1592 (possibly as
early as 1589). Publication in 1592 may have been
occasioned by the notoriety (for debauchery and
drunkeness) of Robert Greene's death.

In any event, the pamphlet is addressed to the
'gentlemen' (playwriters and fellow 'University
Wits,' Christopher Marlowe, Thomas Nashe and
George Peele), who are warned not to trust actors.
The long-winded pamphlet never uses the name
Shake-speare in any form. The excerpted passage
reads,

> Base minded men, all three of you, if by my miserie you
> be not warned: ...those Puppets (I meane) that spake from
> our mouths, those Antics garnisht in our colours... Yes
> trust them not: for there is an vpstart Crow, that with his
> *Tygers hart wrapt in a Players hyde*, supposes he is well
> able to bombast out a blanke verse as the best of you; and
> being an absolute *Iohannes factotum*, is in his owne

conceyte the only Shake-scene in a countrey. O that I might entreat your rare wits to be imploied in more profitable courses: & let those Apes imitate your past excellence, and neuer more aquaint them with your admired intentions.

From the preceding, which does not include the words Shake-speare or Shaksper anywhere, scholars have adduced that Will Shaksper was known as a playwright, an actor, or both by 1592. This is a stretch no rubber band is capable of making. Reasons that dispute 'Groats-worth' refers to Shake-speare or Shaksper as a playwright, actor or both follow:

1. *'Groats-worth'* is addressed to dramatists, to warn dramatists against actors changing the words and meaning of the dramatist. *'Groats-worth'* never considers the 'upstart Crow' to be a dramatist or to have a reputation as a writer.

2. The Shake-speare plays and attitude toward acting are decidedly opposed to bombast. See Hamlet's speech to the actors (p. 47), which begins "Speak the speech, I pray you, as I pronounced it to you, trippingly on the tongue: but if you mouth it..." A describtion of Shake-speare as a bombastic actor goes against everything in the writings. This is not Shake-speare's way or a likely characterization of how those who wrote the plays would act on stage.

3. Will Shaksper was never known as an actor. We believe his function was prompter-writer and 'artistic director.' Shaksper's limited stage acting was incidental to his true role (prompting) and was for minor parts (fill in). Scholars, to date, have not determined which acting Company Shaksper was affiliated with in 1592 (the year 'Groats-worth' was published), much less whether he had by then some reputation.

4 In 1592, the name Shake-speare had never appeared as author on any play, poem, or reference to Will Shaksper (not even in *'Groats-worth')*. The first time the name appeared as author of a play was in 1598. A name not used in 1592 is inconsistent with the bearer of the name having a reputation.

5. The case has been made for the difference in literal meaning and pronunciation of the names Shaksper (Shaxper) and Shake-speare (Sheik-spair). Will Shaksper used variants of Shaxsper (without an 'e' in the first syllable), during his life. *'Groats-worth'* makes no reference to Shaksper.

6. *'Groats-worth'* quotes in modified form, the line "Tygers hart wrapt in a Players hyde." If the quote is from Shake-speare, the anti-bombast acting stylist, *'Groats-worth'* is borrowing from a fellow writer-ally to disparage the 'upstart Crow.'

'Tigers heart' to describe a cruel woman, like 'lion hearted' to describe a strong man, were familiar metaphors in Elizabethan times. These metaphors can be found in works dating to the 1570s and earlier. The phrase *"Tygers hart wrapt in a Players hyde"* may have been first used on stage in *Henry VI*, or added to *Henry VI* after Shake-speare read *Groats-worth of Witte*. Certainly the play was printed after (1594) the pamphlet was printed (1592). Shake-speare has often been accused of incorporating anything of note into the works.

The *'Groats-worth'* passage refers to an unnamed actor (upstart Crow) put down as a mad woman with an actor's exterior (Tyger's hart...), who supposes he can improvise on stage (bombast out blanke verse), in the quality of you writers (as the best of you), and dabbling in many things (Johannes factotum), is conceited enough to think he's the only scene stealer (Shake-scene) in the country.

Who was/were (in 1592 or earlier) the upstart, conceited actor, with little appreciation of play-wrights, who dabbled in other things? Two names that come to mind are Edward Alleyn and Will Kempe. Alleyn played all his roles as an extension of himself, was an entrepreneur-company manager, and made his fortune at the expense of writers and actors. Will Kempe was notorious for the liberties he took with script.

In any event, the lines in question do not refer to any playwright (including Shaksper). Ben Jonson, and perhaps other playrights, credited Shaksper with making it possible to receive a Chamberlain's Men performance.

Certainly it is fanciful to conclude from Chettle's Chuckle (Greene's *Groats-worth of Witte*), that Will Shaksper was an actor of note in 1592. What is documented about Shaksper in 1592, is that he loaned money (£7) to John Clayton, yeoman of Wellington. The loan was acknowledged in Cheapside, near the Boar's Head Inn, scene of diversion for Falstaff and Prince Hal.

Robert Greene is one of the authors included by Kunitz and Haycraft in *British Authors Before 1800*. In discussing *'Groats-worth'* they say,

> A *Groatsworth of Wit* contains the supposed attack on Shakespeare, coupled with appeals to Marlowe, Peele, and Nashe to reform their wicked lives. It would be natural that a man of a higher social class, with a university background, should resent the success of a nobody. But an examination of the famous passage "upstart crow beautified with our feathers" who is "in his own conceyte the only shake-scene in the countrey" makes it probable that the person alluded to is some unnamed actor, not any of Greene's fellow dramatists.

The preceding ten myths have been used many times over the centuries. They have been the basis of much embroidery and pseudobiography. When factual material has disagreed with the myths, it has been ignored.

APPENDIX B

SHAKSPER BIOGRAPHY

It is important to re-evaluate the standard biography of Will Shaksper. To do this we have selected and briefly excerpted from a well written / researched version presented in the *World Book Encyclopedia*. This extensive, beautifully illustrated article by Frank S. Wadsworth, presents a balanced traditional version of the life of the *Bard*.

We have re-arranged excerpts into sections on Shake-speare's Work, Shaksper Biography and Shake-speare Literary Life. Boldface is added for emphasis. Comments are in square brackets.

Frank S. Wadsworth is Professor of Literature Emeritus at the State University of New York, College at Purchase. He is author of *The Poacher from Stratford*.

SHAKE-SPEARE'S WORK

Shakespeare understood people as few other artists have. ...plays contain vivid characters from many walks of life. Kings, pickpockets, drunkards, generals, hired killers, shepherds, and philosophers all mingle... had knowledge in a wide variety of other subjects... music, the law, the Bible, military science, the stage, art, politics, the sea, history, hunting, woodcraft, and sports. Yet as far as scholars know,

Shakespeare had **no professional experience in any field except the theater**...

Shakespeare also contributed greatly to the development of the English language... freely experimented with grammar and vocabulary and so helped prevent literary English from becoming fixed and artificial...

Many words and phrases from Shakespeare... have become part of our everyday speech. ...Shakespeare originated... *fair play, a foregone conclusion, catch cold*, and *disgraceful conduct*. ... invented such common words as *assassination, bump, eventful*, and *lonely*. ...Many people can identify lines and passages as Shakespeare ...Examples include "To be, or not to be," "Friends, Romans, countrymen, lend me your ears," and "A horse! A horse! my kingdom for a horse!" ...jealousy as "the green-eyed monster"... ingratitude as "sharper than a serpent's tooth"...

During the Elizabethan Age, the English cared little about keeping biographical information unrelated to the affairs of the church or state... However, a number of records exist that deal with Shakespeare's [**Shaksper's non-literary**] life. Although these records are few and incomplete by modern standards, they provide much information...

SHAKSPER BIOGRAPHY

Born in Stratford in 1564... baptism on April 26... **probably** attended the Stratford grammar school with other boys of his class... In November 1582... received a license to marry Anne Hathaway... Shakespeare [**Shaksper**] was 18... Anne was 26... first child Susanna, was baptised on May 26, 1583... No significant factual information exists... between Feb. 2, 1585 and 1592... [**then**] Sometime after he arrived in London, **probably** joined one of the city's repertory theater companies... do not know which theater company or companies Shakespeare [**Shaksper**] joined before 1594. But he was a *sharer* (stockholder) of a company called the Lord Chamberlain's Men in 1594[?]. The evidence consists of a record of payment to Shakespeare and his fellow actors for performances by the company at Queen Elizabeth's court... [**Questions about the authenticity/accuracy of this record are presented in Appendix A**]. ...From 1594 to 1608 Shakespeare [**Shaksper**] was fully involved in the London theater world. ...stockholder and actor... ...by the late 1590's... he had become prosperous. In 1597, he purchased New Place, one of the two largest houses in Stratford. Shakespeare [**Shaksper**] obviously remained a Stratford man at heart... Records of business dealings and of minor lawsuits reveal that he preferred to invest most of his money in Stratford rather than in London. ...Shakespeare [**Shaksper**] purchased a house in the Blackfriars district of London in 1613. The evidence thus suggests that Shakespeare [**Shaksper**] gradually reduced his activity in London rather than ending it abruptly. ...must have divided his time between... Stratford... [and] ... London....had lodgings in London at least to 1604 and **probably** until 1611. ...family events... daughter Susana's marriage in 1607... mother's death in 1608 would certainly have called him back to Stratford... 1616... Judith married... Six weeks later, Shakespeare [**Shaksper**] revised his will [**almost disinheriting Judith**]. Within a month he died. He was buried inside the Stratford parish church. His monument records the day of his **death as April 23, the generally accepted day of his birth**. [?] [**No mention of interesting will and contents**].

SHAKE-SPEARE LITERARY LIFE

...There is some indication that Shakespeare had become well known in London theatrical life by 1592. That year, a pamphlet appeared with an apparent reference to [**quote from**] Shake-speare... [**The Wadsworth description of Greene's pamphlet and Chettle's apology are omitted and these items are discussed in Appendix A**] ...From mid-1592 to 1594, London authorities often closed the public theaters because of repeated outbreaks of plague. The need for new plays declined. At this time Shakespeare **began to write [possibly wrote/rewrote]** poems... Shakespeare perhaps believed that by writing poems he might be able to win the praise that mere playwriting never received... In 1593, Shakespeare's long poem *Venus and Adonis* was printed by Richard Field, a **[Shaksper]** Stratford neighbor who had become a London printer... dedicated   to 19-year-old Henry Wriothesley, the Earl of Southampton. The poet may have believed the dedication would win him the earl's favor and support... Field printed Shakes-peare's next long poem, *The Rape of Lucrece*, in 1594... also dedicated to Southampton... wording of the dedication **suggests the possibility**... the young nobleman rewarded [Shaksper]... probably financial[ly]... for dedication of *Venus and Adonis*.

[Scholarly attempts to date the sequence and time of writing/re-writing the Shake-speare plays has profound effects on Shake-speare's perceived literary biography.]

...The Sonnets... In the late 1500's it was fashionable for English **gentlemen** authors to write sequences of sonnets. Some sequences of sonnets followed a narrative pattern that was autobiographical in varying degrees. For this reason scholars have tried to learn about Shakespeare's life from his sonnets. But they have reached no general agreement on the autobiographical information that the poems may contain... ...Shakespeare probably wrote the sonnets over a period of several years though their dates are not clear. He wrote the poems in three units of four lines each concluding *couplet* [two-line unit]. Shakespeare's sonnets rhyme *abab cdcd efef gg*.

COMMENT

The preceding excerpts present what is known about Shaksper's personal life and the literary life of Shake-speare. From these minimal facts, full length biographies have been attempted. To do this, assumptions galore have to be made about Shaksper and the Elizabethan era. The greatest assumption (myth) is that Shaksper was the sole author of the Shake-speare works.

Winston Churchill, when confronted with the Oxfordian theory, indicated that he didn't like tampering with his boyhood myths (traditional Shake-speare story). Churchill is not alone.

Gary Taylor, in the Introduction to *Reinventing Shakespeare*, presents an interesting example of the Shaksper myth:

> For a while Shakespeare reinvented himself almost every day. He had to; he was an actor. In the Elizabethan repertory system, he might be expected to perform in six different plays on six consecutive days. Many times he would rehearse one play in the morning and perform another that afternoon. On most days he probably played more than one character; Elizabethan actors doubled, tripled, quadrupled roles, their versatility helping to hold down costs.

> When he was not acting in plays he was writing them. Like actors, Elizabethan playwrights were encouraged to demonstrate their adaptability. In less than twenty-four months at the turn of the seventeenth century Shakespeare wrote *Much adoe about Nothing, The Life of Henry the Fift, The Tragedie of Julius Caeser, As you Like it,* and *The Tragedie of Hamlet Prince of Denmarke,* probably in that order, probably one after another. Even before he finished one play he had begun thinking about or even writing the next; toward the end of *Henry the Fift* he borrowed images from the same pages of Plutarch that he would use as source material for *Julius Caesar*. As an

actor he needed to become only two or three characters per play; as a playwright he had to perform all the parts in his head, momentarily recreating himself in the image of each. He juggled selves.

He did not stop juggling when he stepped out of the theatre. "All the world's a stage," he wrote; he also wrote, "my nature is subdue'd / To what it works in, like the dyers hand." He could not stop being an actor any more than the Globe itself could stop being a theatre. Like his characters, he played his part in family burials and marriages; he loaned money, bought property, invested venture capital, sued people, testified in court. He delighted civil audiences in an open-air theatre in the suburbs; he deferred to rowdy crowds indoors at court. He doubled one set of commitments in metropolitan London with another set in provincial Stratford-upon-Avon, like two roles in one play, like plot and subplot, like art and nature. He embodied mutability.

But gradually the pace of metamorphosis began to slow. At some time between 1603 and 1610 he seems to have stopped acting. After 1606 he wrote fewer plays; increasingly often, he collaborated with other writers. After 1608 he spent less and less time in London. After 1613 he stopped writing and commuting; geographically and imaginatively his world contracted. Finally on April 23, 1616, he stopped reinventing himself altogether, He was buried two days later.

We have been reinventing him ever since [**if not initially**].

Myths are powerful and hypnotic in their nature. Many a biography and history book contain a fair amount of myth. We can only stop re-inventing Shake-speare, when we start with the question, 'Who Were Shake-speare?'

APPENDIX C

RESEARCH APLENTY

The Internet and computer age of the twenty-first century should alter investigation into the authorship of Shake-speare's works. It is currently possible to inexpensively publish (on CD-rom) fascimile versions of all applicable Shake-speare source materials. The Internet is already being used by organizations and individual scholars to disseminate information on Shake-speare. The works of many Elizabethan authors are available on the Internet and CD-rom. Scholars are developing computer programs to analyze the text of writers for authorial characteristics. The future danger will be to avoid being overcome by quantity of data, rather than the quality of results.

Computerized text analysis. This approach has been used by Ward Elliot and Robert Valenza at Claremont College. It would be of value to ascertain the provenance of works such as the play *Sir Thomas More*, the poem *Romeus and Juliet*, the *'Phaeton'* sonnet, etc. The play, *Sir Thomas More*, may be the closest we have to a Shake-speare fair copy. Such a possibility is worth further research.

There are a great many questions about the validity of computerized text analysis to the Shake-speare works. First there are questions about the works themselves, and the versions of such used in computer testing. Most editions of the Shake-speare Sonnets make significant changes to the original edition (1609). For example, Sonnet one, line two, contains the word *Rose* (possibly for Henry Wriothesley and pronounced Rose-ly). This is not italicized or capitalized in most editions. Should one use any edition other than the original authoritative texts for computer analysis?

Can any computer program tell which sections of the Shake-speare works are by which original hand? Can any computer program distinguish what is good, bad, or great writing in the Shake-speare works? Does indiscrimate use of a modern edition of Shake-speare for computer text analysis corrupt the results obtained? How much text provides a valid sample for statistical purposes (one line, one sonnet, ten pages, etc.)?

Once one has accurate, valid samples of Shake-speare works, there are questions about computer programs and techniques to consider. These include: Do we have several different logical test approaches that consistently produce similar statistically valid answers on works of a wide range of Elizabethan authors? Can results of such computer analysis be independently tested and evaluated by statisticians?

It is beyond the scope of this book to answer these questions. However, refining such computer testing techniques and independently verifying results should yield valuable results in the future.

Old fashioned hand-analysis of materials. We have previously discussed two samples of this approach; Roger Stritmatter's ongoing work on the Oxford 'Geneva' Bible at the Folger Library, and Charles Hamilton's more fanciful work on the *Last Will and Testament* of Will Shaksper.

The 'Geneva' Bible, purchased in 1589, by Edward de Vere, 17th Earl of Oxford, has been in the Folger Library, Washington D.C., since 1924. This Bible is possibly one of the Bibles used as a reference in creating the Shake-speare works. *The Reader's Encyclopedia of Shakespeare* states:

> The nature and extent of Shakespeare's use of the Bible has been the subject of much speculation resulting in widely divergent opinions. The most balanced discussion is that of Richmond Noble in his Shakespeare's Biblical Knowledge (1935) in which the author gives careful consideration to earlier scholarship in addition to presenting his own conclusions. With regard to the version used, Noble offers a corrective to the once-prevalent view that Shakespeare relied almost exclusively on the Genevan version. It now appears that he used the Bishops' Bible for his earlier plays and that he subsequently tended to rely more heavily on the Genevan Bible. For the New Testament he apparently used Lawrence Thomson's revision (1576) rather than the original Genevan text. His quotations of the Psalms correspond most closely to that of the 1540 edition of the Great Bible; the Book of Common Prayer which, with minor changes, drew its Scriptural texts from the Great Bible was more likely his immediate source.

Be that as it may, de Vere's 'Geneva' Bible contains numerous marked passages and marginal notes. A high percentage of such obscure passages has been found to have been used in the Shake-speare plays. How many hands performed this marking and notation (de Vere, Shaksper, others)? It would be of value if some of the pages were published or made available for research through the Internet.

Charles Hamilton's *In Search of Shakespeare*, has made a case for Will Shaksper, himself writing his *Last Will and Testament*. If so, this is an important discovery; for aside from signatures, this would be the only known document in Shaksper's hand. The will might be analyzed for new insights. After reviewing available contemporary wills, letters and documents of Shaksper's time (including the handwriting of family members such as Dr. Hall), the validity of Shaksper preparing his own will should be able to be confirmed by research and independent handwriting analysis.

Millions of documents have been studied in the last century to find information related to Will Shaksper. The focus of this study on Shaksper may have bypassed valuable information on Oxford's Men, Oxford's Boys, the provenance of plays which were produced earlier than 1589, and those associated with the Shake-speare canon through Edward de Vere (Arthur Golding, Mary Browne, de Vere's daughters and first cousin Horatio Vere, etc.). I have included in the list, Mary Browne, daughter of Viscount Anthony Montagu, and wife of the 2nd

Earl of Southampton. The following excerpy is from G. P. V. Akrigg's *Shakespeare and the Earl of Southampton*:

...on July 30 [1550] he died in London... He left numerous daughters and one son, Henry, now at the age of five became the second Earl of Southampton. The new earl being a minor, passed into the custody of the royal Master of the Wards. The Master, to raise revenue for the Crown, customarily sold wardships to the highest bidders, who then set about administering their wards' estates in the manner which would yield them the highest returns on their investment...

The Earl of Southampton's country seat at Tichfield became, like so many of the great houses of the Catholic English nobility, a bastion of Catholicism. Many a priest was harbored there before slipping away to [Cowdray]... the home of Anthony Browne, first Viscount Montegu. Not surprisingly, when the Earl married on February 19th, 1566, his bride was Montagu's thirteen year old daughter, Mary...

...An English earl [Southampton] who had asked a Roman Catholic bishop whether or not he should obey the Queen had to be severely punished. Arrested at the end of October 1571, the second Earl of Southampton was packed off to the Tower of London... During his second year in the Tower, Southampton redoubled his efforts to secure his release. Writing to William Cecil, Lord Burghley...[and others finally had an effect]... On May 1st, 1573, the Privy Council released Southampton from the Tower... The Countess was pregnant and the time of her delivery were drawing near. On October 6th, 1573, she gave birth to a son [Henry future 3rd Earl of Southampton]...

[The 2nd Earl] Tetchy, ill-tempered and proud, both weak and obstinate, [possibly bisexual] he was no doubt

something less than a perfect husband. His wife...
[Countess Mary] was on her way to becoming the self-
willed, self pitying, sensuous woman of her middle years...
The storm broke in 1580 when the Earl learned that his
wife had been seen with Donesame at Dogmersfield under
circumstances that left him in no doubt that the man was
her lover. In his fury the Earl broke not only with her but
with her family. An entry in the register of the Privy
Council indicates that, as with the Montagues and
Capulets, so with the Montagus and Wriothesleys, the
servants took up the family quarrel...

This all relates to Mary Browne, mother of the 3rd
Earl of Southampton, later married to Sir Thomas
Heneage, Vice Chamberlain. It's a pity there is not
a biography of Mary Browne. One wonders also
about the relationship (which could date back to
childhood) of Mary Browne and Edward de Vere.
Could the rumor about the 3rd Earl's parents being
Queen Elizabeth and de Vere, be a distortion?
Could de Vere (distant from his wife) and Mary
Browne (with her husband in the Tower for two
plus years) have had a more intimate relationship?

Another worthy area of study is Thomas Nashe and
his writings such as *Strange News* (1592). The Will
Monox (*Mon* Ox or My Ox) that Nashe writes about
could certainly be Edward de Vere, Earl of Oxford.

More can be studied about the Clayton suit and
Shaksper's moneylending. Many scholars try to
write off this suit since a 'William Shakespeare'
lived in Bedfordshire. This is nonsense since the
particulars of the loan took place in London at the
time Shakspere was there. The Bedfordshire man

did not even spell or pronounce his name as did Shaksper.

In any event, there is much material for re-evaluation and re-examination related to the authorship of the Shake-speare works.

Computer publication and dissemination of research. Scholars are already using the Internet to provide access and feedback related to the Shake-speare authorship. There are Stratfordian and Oxfordian information and propaganda centers. An example of information dissemination is the work which Alan Nelson is undertaking. His Internet address is:
http://violet.berkeley.edu~ ahnelson
Nelson is doing research into the biography of Edward de Vere and his family as well as orthography.

Computer publication / dissemination through the Internet, as well as CD publication should become a greater research tool in the coming years. Think of a time when all the works / documents related to Shake-speare and Elizabethan contemporaries would be available (in facsimile) with modern transcriptions to interactively view, select, perform internal analysis (with a package of provided tools) on your garden variety PC equivalent. It is technically possible right now!

Current computer sources on Shaksper, de Vere and other Shake-speare authorship candidates are marred by their partisan bias. Too much time is spent disparaging the personal traits of individuals. The fact that Shaksper was a moneylender, minor business man, grain hoarder or hated his wife, doesn't relate at all to whether he co-authored the Shake-speare works.

De Vere and his family (father and son) may have been wanton voluptuaries, may have been terrible husbands, and Edward may have dissipated his fortune foolishly. This does not disqualify co-authorship.

De Vere's letter writing style should not be taken as an indication of his playwriting and poetry style. Writers adapt their style / affectations to the media, project, and formality of the work at hand. De Vere's lifestyle and letters have minimal bearing on whether de Vere co-authored the Shake-speare works.

Once the authorship myths about Shake-speare are cast aside, serious new ground can be broken on the composite authorship of the Shake-speare works. New and more complete availability of original source materials will be provided by computer technology. Re-evaluation of these materials and the discovery of new sources will help further unlock the authorship mysteries.

The future will provide more information to unequivocably answer the question of 'Who Were Shake-speare?'

APPENDIX D

ON SHAKE-SPEARE CLAIMANTS

Early in this text, it was indicated that over 100 claimants have been proposed over the centuries as the writer, William Shake-speare. The Elizabethan era was a time of much collaboration and borrowing of intellectual properties. Our current attitude toward plagiarism is less tolerant than that held in the sixteenth century.

Many intelligent people, over several hundred years, have found Will Shaksper an unlikely candidate for the sole authorship of the Shake-speare works. A number of these questioners have been well known writers or actors who have tried to square the 'myth' with their observations. Some of the reasons for this doubt follow:

1. Will Shaksper, born in 1565, was too young to have written the early plays, which can be dated to the 1580's or before.

2. The plays, poems and sonnets written by 1595, when Will was thirty, amount to an enormous portion of Shake-speare's output. To achieve this in a period of less than ten years, without prior preparation, having limited education and bereft of worldly

experience, in a new environment (other than provincial Stratford) is most unlikely.

3. The convincing Italian and continental backdrops of many plays speaks of travel not experienced by Shaksper. There is also corresponding use of foreign language and terms in the plays.

4. The noble personages and depictions of nobility in the plays attests to firsthand experience Will Shaksper did not possess.

5. The education (medicine, sports, flowers, law, military matters, marine terms, etc.) and the exceedingly large vocabulary (30,000 words) in a time of no dictionaries are non-intuitive (learned skills) which do not square with Shaksper's grammar school education.

6. The lack of serious personal censorship of Will Shaksper's often politically explosive work makes one wonder about who protected him. It would have taken political clout Will did not have to survive offending the Old-castle relatives and other sensitive nobles.

This valid scepticism has led to some elaborate and far-fetched theories. The leading person proposed for sole authorship of Shake-speare's works, in the twentieth century, is Edward de Vere, 17th Earl of Oxford. Four additional men, Francis Bacon, Christopher Marlowe, the Earl of Rutland (fifth), and the Earl of Derby (sixth) have proponents as the *Bard*.

Francis Bacon, 1561-1626, was a well known philosopher, essayist, and statesman. There is no direct evidence of Bacon's involvement in theater, acting, or playwrighting, much less being Shakespeare. One wonders why the contributors to the *First Folio* who memorialized the *Bard* as deceased, would do so if he were alive, as Bacon was in 1623.

Christopher Marlowe, 1564-1593, was murdered in Deptford, possibly for political reasons. Theories about Marlowe living and writing after his murder can be traced back to a fanciful novel. The substansive proof is that Marlowe died young, and did not collaborate with anyone from the grave or beyond.

Roger Manners, the fifth Earl of Rutland, ?-1612, was a courtly gentleman. However, there is no evidence that he wrote literature of any kind.

William Stanley, the sixth Earl of Derby, 1561-1642, was a nobleman of rank. Perhaps the richest man in England in his time and potentially in line for the throne, he had to watch his step. Derby married Edward de Vere's daughter Susan. Derby gave up patronage of Strange's Men when the Queen formed and absorbed Derby's actors into the Queen's Men. It is difficult to imagine Derby as a major contributor since he lived until 1642. Shakespeare works stopped being written decades earlier. Derby did not contribute to the *First Folio* project.

Figure 47 is a partial list of claimants who have
been put forward as sole or partial authors of the
Shake-speare works. The list is long. Perhaps some
in the list made some minor contributions to the
Shake-speare canon.

SHAKE-SPEARE AUTHORSHIP CLAIMANTS

Alexander, William Earl of Sterling
Bacon, Anthony - brother of Francis
Barnes, Barnabe
Barnfield, Richard
Bernard, Sir John
Blount, Sir Charles, Lord Mountjoy
Burbage, Richard
Burton, Robert
Butts, William
Cecil, Robert, Earl of Salisbury
Chettle, Henry
Daniel, Samuel
Dekker, Thomas
Devereux, Robert, 2nd Earl of Essex
Devereux, Walter, 1st Earl of Essex
Donne, John
Drayton, Michael
Dyer, Sir Edward
Elizabeth I, Queen
Ferrers, Henry
Fletcher, John
Florio, John
Florio, Michelangelo - father of John
Greene, Robert
Griffin, Bartholomew
Heywood, Thomas
Jesuits, the

Jonson, Ben
Kyd, Thomas
Lodge, Thomas
Lyly, John
Mary, Queen of Scots
Middleton, Thomas
Munday, Anthony
Nashe, Thomas
Paget, Henry, Lord
Peele, George
Porter, Henry
Raleigh, Sir Walter
Rosicrucians, the
Sackville, Thomas, Lord Buckhurst
Shirley, Sir Anthony
Sidney, Eliz., Countess of Rutland
Sidney, Mary, Countess of Pembroke
Sidney, Sir Philip
Smith, Wentworth
Spenser, Edmund
Warner, William
Watson, Thomas
Webster, John
Whateley, Anne
Wilson, Robert
Wolsey, Thomas, Cardinal
Wriothesley, Henry, Earl of Southampton

47. Shake-speare Authorship Claimants.

We know that Will Shaksper did go to London and
become an important member of the Chamberlain's
and King's Men. His role was not that of a major
actor but that of prompter-artistic director and as
writer / co-writer of the Shake-speare plays and

poems. The Chamberlain's-King's Men put on a great number of non-Shake-speare plays.

Edward de Vere, the 17th Earl of Oxford, was a patron of acting companies, playwright, poet, occasional actor and a mainstay of the London theatrical community. His early plays, travel, library, contacts, education, and personal experience enabled him to begin the writing and traditions which flowered in the Shake-speare works.

Men such as Christopher Marlowe, Thomas Kyd, John Lyly, Anthony Munday and John Fletcher participated in play writing, updating, editing and contributing plays to either Oxford's Men, or the Chamberlain's-King's Men.

Playwrights, scribes, printers, and actors, affected what has come down to us as 'by Shake-speare.'

To propose sole authorship (by any claimant) of the Shake-speare works, in the face of what is known about Elizabethan theater and how the Shake-speare works evolved over time, is contrary to the facts and disregards logic / common sense.

William Shaksper and Edward de Vere were in London during the creation / development of the Shake-speare plays and poetry. Shaksper came on the scene late and was ill equipped to write the Shake-speare works by himself. Shaksper's limitations have been the major cause for seeking alternative writers for the Shake-speare works.

If there really were another sole author of the works, it becomes difficult to explain Shaksper's long-term association with the Chamberlain's and King's Men as Company owner and theatres owner (Globe and Blackfriar's). A straw man? Not likely.

De Vere's active co-participation with Shaksper in creating the Shake-speare works solves many of the questions posed about Shaksper capacity as a sole author.

Shaksper and de Vere were there, and were the main co-writers. No other person can be reasonably presented as a co-writer to Shaksper and de Vere. Other candidates have <u>not</u> been credibly tied to Shaksper (or de Vere) as a co-writer.

The candidates bandied about are – too old, too young, died too early, did not have the necessary tools, were not in London at the appropriate time, etc., to have been a major co-writer of the Shake-speare works.

Thus we have flights of fancy which include: Marlowe not dying in 1593, but living on in Europe and sending his works to London; Bacon leaving all sorts of cryptography to indicate his authorship; and Queen Elizabeth's face being the model for the infamous Droeshout portrait in the *First Folio*.

Once co-authorship is considered, the fantasy recedes, and the true authors are revealed.

SELECTED BIBLIOGRAPHY

(includes INTERNET sources)

The Reader's Encyclopedia of Shakespeare. Edited by Oscar James Campbell. Associate editor: Edward G. Quinn. New York, Crowell, 1966.

The Harvard Concordance to Shakespeare. Marvin Spevack, editor. Cambridge, Mass., Belknap Press of Harvard University Press, 1973.

Shakespeare's Plays in Quarto: a facsimile edition of copies primarily from the Henry E. Huntington Library. Shakespeare, William. Edited, with introduction and notes, by Michael J.B. Allen and Kenneth Muir. University of Calif. Pr., c1981.

Shakespeare's Poems: a facsimile of the earliest editions, by William Shakespeare. New Haven, Published for the Elizabethan Club [by] Yale University Press, 1964.

British Authors Before 1800; a biographical dictionary. Edited by Stanley J. Kunitz and Howard Haycraft. New York, Wilson, 1952.

The Compact Edition of the Oxford English Dictionary: complete text reproduced micrographically. Uniform title: A new English dictionary on historical principles. New York : Oxford University Press, c1971.

The Oxford English Dictionary. Oxford: Clarendon Press, 1991. Edition: 2nd ed. / prepared by J.A. Simpson and E.S.C. Weiner.

Shakespeare's Pronunciation, by Helge Kökeritz. Yale University Press, 1953.

The Mysterious William Shakespeare: the myth and the reality, Charlton Ogburn. McLean, Vir.: EPM Publications, Inc., c1984.

The Friendly Shakespeare: a thoroughly painless guide to the best of the bard, by Norrie Epstein. New York: Penguin Books, 1994.

Shakespeare's Plays in the Order of Their Writing, a study based on the records of the court revels and historic allusions, by Eva Turner Clark. London, Cecil Palmer, 1930.

The Elizabethan Stage, by E. K. Chambers. Oxford: Clarendon Press, 1951. Revised edition.

A Shakespeare Companion, 1564-1964, by F. E. Halliday. New York: Schocken Books, 1964.

The Shakespearean Stage, 1574-1642, by Andrew Gurr. Cambridge; New York: Cambridge University Press, 1992. 3rd edition.

Shakespeare's Professional Skills, by Nevill Coghill. Cambridge [Eng.] University Press, 1964.

The Works of William Shakespeare: in reduced facsimile from the famous first folio edition of 1623. With an introduction by J. O. Halliwell-Phillipps. New York: Funk & Wagnalls, 1887. First edition.

Shakespeare's Hamlet, the Second Quarto, 1604: reproduced in facsimile from the copy in the Huntington Library, with an introduction by Oscar James Campbell. San Marino, CA: 1938.

Shakespeare's Use of the Arts of Language, by Sister Miriam Joseph. N. Y., Columbia University Press, 1947.

In Search of Shakespeare: a reconnaissance into the poet's life and handwriting, by Charles Hamilton., San Diego: Harcourt Brace Jovanovich, c1985. 1st ed.

Brooke's "Romeus and Juliet," being the original of Shakespeare's "Romeo and Juliet" / newly edited by J. J. Munro. Philadelphia: R. West, 1978.

INTERNET SOURCES

MIT (Massachusetts Institute of Technology) - A source of the complete works, discussion group, Internet Shakespeare Resources, Bartlett's familiar Shakespearean quotes, etc.
      http:the-tech.mit.edu/Shakespeare

Matty Farrows Shakespeare search engine (fast, easy searches of the complete works.
      http://www.gs.usyd.edu.au/~matty/Shakespeare/test.html

Shakespeare Links - A source to sites including complete works (4), varied play editions, academic resources, meta resources, companies, festivals, authorship (Shaksper, de Vere, Bacon, etc.), movies and miscellany.
    http://www.ludweb.com/msff/sonnets/links.html

The Shakespeare Authorship Page - Dedicated to proving that "Shakespeare was Shakespeare."
    http://www.bcpl.lib.md.us/~tross/ws

Shakespeare Oxford Society Home Page - Information on Edward Oxford and from the 'Oxfordian' persective.
    http:www.shakespeare-oxford.com

Lyly, Nashe and other Elizabethan writers - biography, criticism and works.
    http://www.alchemyweb.com/~alchemy/englit/renlit

INDEX